An Introduction to Catholic Theology

edited by

Richard Lennan

PAULIST PRESS
New York/Mahwah, N.J.

The Publisher gratefully acknowledges use of the following: Excerpt from "Triptych" from *Selected Poems 1966–1987* by Seamus Heaney. Copyright 1990 by Seamus Heaney. Reprinted by permission of Farrar, Straus & Giroux, Inc. and Faber and Faber, Ltd. Excerpts from *The Documents of Vatican II* (Dominican Publications, copyright 1996), edited by Austin Flannery. Reprinted by permission of Dominican Publications.

Nihil Obstat: Rev. B. Byron, D.D., M.Th.

Imprimatur: Cardinal E. B. Clancy, A.C., Archbishop of Sydney

Date: November 3, 1997

The Nihil Obstat and Imprimatur are a declaration that a book or pamphlet is considered to be free from doctrinal or moral error. It is not necessarily implied that those who have granted them agree with the contents, opinions or statements expressed.

Cover design by Cindy Dunne

Book design by Theresa M. Sparacio

Library of Congress Cataloging-in-Publication Data

An introduction to Catholic theology / edited by Richard Lennan.
    p.   cm.
    Includes bibliographical references and index.
    ISBN 0–8091–3808–5 (alk. paper)
    1. Catholic Church—Doctrines. 2. Theology, Doctrinal—Introductions. I. Lennan, Richard.
BX1751.2.I58   1998
230′.2—dc21   98–20642
                                                   CIP

Published by Paulist Press
997 Macarthur Boulevard
Mahwah, New Jersey 07430

Printed and bound in the
United States of America

Distributed in Australia by
Rainbow Book Agencies Pty. Ltd/
Word of Life Distributors
303 Arthur Street
Fairfield, VIC 3078

CONTENTS

PREFACE

This book has grown out of the authors' concern for the needs of university and college students who are beginning their study of theology. We have in mind students like those in our degree program at the Catholic Institute of Sydney, Australia. We want to offer these students an integrated understanding of the various theological disciplines they will encounter, give them access to some of the best contemporary insights into Catholic theology, and assist them as they begin to engage in theological inquiry for themselves. In so doing, we hope they will come to appreciate what is distinctive about Catholic theology in the contemporary intellectual world.

With such aims, it is clear that this book could not have been written by one person. To be true to its claim to be an introduction to Catholic theology, this book required the insights of philosophers, biblical scholars, systematic theologians, ethicists, and pastoral theologians. In addition, we have tried to ensure that the book is an integrated text and not merely a collection of chapters. Its production has involved a genuine academic collaboration in which all of the authors were involved at each stage of the planning, writing, and final editing. Hence, while authorship of each chapter can be ascribed to a particular individual (and is so ascribed in our biographical notes below), it is also true that each of us has had our views and positions tested by our peers, and that the final form of each chapter is the work of several hands.

We believe this book captures something of the spirit and approach to theology that has developed at the Catholic Institute of Sydney. It reflects our concern for the academic integrity of our programs and our desire to be of service to our students beyond the confines of the lecture

1

room or the individual course unit. We hope our students will benefit as our teaching incorporates the insights we have gained from this collaborative effort. We hope this work will not only be an appropriate textbook for theology courses, but will also be of interest to a broader public with a view to encouraging theological reflection in both the church and society.

Our book has benefited from the comments of a number of people who read the drafts. Accordingly, we would like to thank Adrian Bartels, Kate Brown, Christine Burke, David Coffey, Tracey Edstein, John Honner, Paul McCabe, Neil Ormerod, June Passlow, Margaret Press, and Michael Putney for their generosity and encouragement. We wish also to acknowledge with thanks the contribution of Kevin Lynch, Kathleen Walsh, and the staff at Paulist Press.

THE AUTHORS:

All of the authors are members of the faculty at the Catholic Institute of Sydney, Australia.

Richard Lennan edited the book and also wrote the Introduction, chapter 1, and the Epilogue. He earned the M.Phil. from the University of Oxford, England, and the Dr.Theol. from the University of Innsbruck, Austria. He has published *The Ecclesiology of Karl Rahner* (Oxford: Clarendon Press, 1995, 1997) and edited *Redefining the Church* (Sydney: E. J. Dwyer, 1995). He heads the Department of Systematic Theology.

Tom Carroll, the author of chapter 2, teaches in the Department of Philosophy. He received the M.Ed. from the Australian Catholic University and both the License and Doctor of Philosophy from the University of Leuven, Belgium. His doctoral dissertation examined Max Scheler's understanding of religious experience.

Gerard Kelly, who wrote chapter 3, teaches in the Department of Systematic Theology. His early theological studies were at the Catholic Institute of Sydney, and his doctoral studies were at the Dominican College of Philosophy and Theology in Ottawa, Canada. He is the author of *Recognition: Advancing Ecumenical Thinking* (New York: Peter Lang, 1996).

Joseph Sobb, S.J., who authored chapter 4 in conjunction with John McSweeney, heads the Department of Biblical Studies and is a member of the Australian College of Education. He received the Ph.D.

from the University of Cambridge, England. His current research is in postexilic prophetic literature.

John McSweeney teaches in the Department of Biblical Studies and is particularly interested in apocalyptic literature. Together with Joseph Sobb, S.J., he wrote chapter 4. Following his theological studies at the Catholic Institute of Sydney, he received the Licentiate in Sacred Scripture from the Pontifical Biblical Institute in Rome.

Gerald Gleeson, who is the author of chapter 5, heads the Department of Philosophy and is a research associate at the John Plunkett Centre for Ethics in Health Care. He has an M.A. from the University of Cambridge, England, and the Ph.D. from the University of Leuven, Belgium. He edited *Priesthood: The Hard Questions* (Sydney: E. J. Dwyer, 1993).

Neil Brown, the author of chapter 6, is president of the Catholic Institute of Sydney and also professor of ethics. His Ph.D. in Sacred Theology is from the Gregorian University in Rome. His books include *The Worth of Persons: A Study in Christian Ethics* (Sydney: CIS, 1983), *Christians in a Pluralist Society* (Sydney: CIS, 1986), and *Spirit of the World* (Sydney: CIS, 1989).

Peter Lynch, who wrote chapter 7, is the deputy president at the Catholic Institute of Sydney and head of the Department of Pastoral Studies. He has the M.A. in Religious Education from Fordham University in New York and the D.Min. from The Catholic University of America. He is the author of *Not Without Hope: Christian Traditions of Grieving* (Sydney: CIS, 1989).

REFERENCES

All references to the Bible are taken from the *New Revised Standard Version* (Copyright 1989, Division of Christian Education of the National Council of the Churches of Christ in the United States of America).

All references to the documents of Vatican II are taken from Austin P. Flannery (ed.), *The Documents of Vatican II,* rev. ed. (Dublin: Dominican Publications, 1996).

INTRODUCTION

Imagine this scene: it is the first day of the academic year, and you are beginning an introductory course in theology. You are about to engage in an area of study that has always been a part of the life of the Christian church and, indeed, has enriched that life immeasurably. You are about to join many other women and men who have sought to understand, to articulate, and to live more fully their relationship with God. In other words, you are about to begin what can be an exciting and fulfilling quest. This book seeks to be a resource and a source of encouragement for your quest.

The first area in which you might need encouragement concerns your decision to study theology. In fact, you might have serious doubts about whether you have made the right choice. You might be anxious that this course will be a tedious examination of documents issued by various popes, or that it will lay down what you must think and do before you can consider yourself a Catholic. Alternatively, you might fear that a course in theology will be about ideas so abstract or complex that they will quickly bore or baffle you.

The fact that students new to the study of theology can approach the subject with such feelings of disquiet says much about the reputation of theology. For some people, theology is a strange activity, one that separates its practitioners from life in the real world and requires that they speculate about the number of angels that can dance on the head of a pin; for others, "theology" is simply the name given to the style of argument designed to show that the Catholic Church is always correct, no matter what its stance on controversial issues; for still oth-

5

ers, theology is the activity engaged in by those who are attracted to abstract concepts and mind-numbing philosophical distinctions.

In order to counter the possibility that such perceptions might dissuade you from the study of theology or even from a study of this book, it is important to stress that theology can be seen in a more favorable light. Those who, like the authors of this book, are enthusiastic about theology emphasize that it is life-enhancing: it is not only about life in the real world, but it can contribute to the endeavor to live that life well. Nonetheless, theologians must remember that theology can go astray if it separates itself from the "reality check" provided by the real lives of real people. Christian theology ought to be particularly aware of the need to remain grounded in real life because it is, as we shall demonstrate, founded on faith in the God who in Jesus Christ shared our human history and who, through the Holy Spirit, remains inseparable from our present and our future.

The fact that human experience is indispensable to our connection with God means that theology cannot be understood without reference to human experience. Accordingly, one of the purposes of this book is to illustrate how human experience and expression are central to theology. In addition to that general aim, this book also has a more particular goal: to introduce readers to the sources, methods, and implications of Catholic theology. Although it is neither a compendium of Catholic beliefs nor an in-depth treatment of any particular theme of Catholic theology, not even of the fundamental themes such as Christology, the Trinity, the church, or creation and eschatology, this book is designed to present the essential principles that characterize an authentically *Catholic* theology.[1]

The Catholic orientation of this book can be seen in the following five features: (1) it prizes human reason and the human desire to seek meaning; (2) it is grounded on the conviction that God can be known by human beings and that God is known by us most fully in Jesus Christ, who offers life to all people; (3) it affirms that God's life-giving presence continues in our history through the Holy Spirit, the Spirit of the risen Jesus, the Spirit who sustains the church and who moves the human heart to be open to God, particularly to the God revealed in the Bible; (4) it recognizes that faith in Jesus Christ is lived within the community of the church and that those in authority within the church—the college of bishops under the leadership of the pope—have a particular responsibility for nurturing the church in unity; and (5) it seeks to articulate that faith in the God of Jesus Christ cannot be separated from engagement with the world; in other words, faith in God affects how one understands oneself, one's neighbor, and the world.

While the book maintains a positive, if not unreflective, exposition of the Catholic flavor of theology, some readers might fear that any narrowing of theology to one particular perspective can be nothing other than a recipe for sectarianism. What, then, can be said not only to allay such a fear, but also to affirm the value of this book's Catholic dimension?

First, we need to recognize that human beings cannot operate outside a tradition: "To be outside all traditions," claims the philosopher Alasdair MacIntyre, "is to be a stranger to enquiry; it is to be in a state of intellectual and moral destitution."[2] The fact that human beings form and operate within traditions means that the mere existence of a "Catholic tradition" is not sufficient proof that Catholic theology is narrow or intolerant.

Although it is certainly true that not everyone sees God, the world, and the human condition in the way that the Catholic tradition does, this fact alone cannot be used to invalidate that tradition. MacIntyre's argument is that the existence of different traditions obliges those traditions to enter into a dialogue in order to search for the truth that might be bigger than any of them. The Catholic tradition would be sectarian only if it refused to engage in a dialogue with other traditions. A fruitful dialogue, however, is possible only when we understand and affirm our own tradition. Without this understanding there is a danger that we might abandon the richness of our tradition for something that glitters but is not gold. This book aims to present the breadth and depth of the Catholic tradition so that the reader might be both enriched by that tradition and better equipped to communicate with people of other traditions.

The second explanation of the specifically Catholic orientation of this book is based on the already-stated principle that Catholic theology is founded on faith in Jesus Christ, who is God's word of life for all people. The fact that this is so means that the Christian must be focused outward. In other words, Catholic Christians ought not to be people who are concerned only with themselves and their own interests; they ought not to be people who delight in their separation from others. Instead, they ought to be people who appreciate that the Spirit of Jesus draws them to others, so that through them God's loving word might be spoken as widely as possible. There is, therefore, a convergence between Mac-Intyre's view of tradition and the dynamic of Christianity itself: both of them are directed toward ensuring that the term *Catholic* is not used to justify either arrogance or bigotry. Our hope for this book is that it will not only benefit Catholics who are seeking to understand and appreciate their own theological heritage, but that it will also be of interest and value for other Christians, for people of other faiths, and indeed for people who do not belong to any specific religious group, but who might be seeking some insight into the Catholic view of the world.

If, then, it is possible to argue that theology is about life in the real world, if it is possible to argue that Catholic theology is not necessarily bigoted, what about the perception that theology is just too difficult to be attractive to other than a few students? Perhaps the best answer to this question comes from the contemporary English theologian Nicholas Lash:

> *Serious theological reflection is always hard work, and its outcome fragmentary, tentative, and (often) quite technical in its quest for appropriate imaginative and conceptual accuracy, not because* God *is complicated, but because we are—and so is the world in which we live. It is not possible without complexity to indicate, or point the way toward, the deep simplicity of the mystery of God.[3]*

The complexity of theology does not mean that the subject is impenetrable. It does mean, however, that the subject can be expected to challenge and stretch us. But as the history of human creativity demonstrates, it is when we are willing to be challenged, when we are willing to be stretched, that we gain a new level of insight into what it is to be human. The authors of this book hope that it does stretch its readers in this way. They hope that those who read it will not only come to appreciate the value of theology, but that they will also find the concepts and language to give an account of their own hope in the mystery of God.

NOTES

[1]For a detailed discussion of the elements of Catholic theology, see Avery Dulles, "Criteria of Catholic Theology," *Communio* 22 (1995): 303–15.

[2]Alasdair MacIntyre, *Whose Justice? Which Rationality?* (Notre Dame, Ind.: University of Notre Dame Press, 1988), 367.

[3]Nicholas Lash, *Easter in Ordinary: Reflections on Human Experience and the Knowledge of God* (London: SCM, 1988; Notre Dame, Ind.: University of Notre Dame Press, 1990), 291.

Chapter One

THEOLOGY

> This chapter provides an overview of theology using a series
> of definitions to identify both the elements and the purpose
> of theology. It examines the relationship between theology
> and the church and surveys past and present ways of doing
> theology. In addition, it discusses the connection between
> theology and spirituality.

The poet and storyteller Rudyard Kipling maintained that *who,
how, where, when,* and *what* provide indispensable assistance to writers. Those same helpers can be used here as we begin to introduce readers to theology and to promote a positive appreciation of theology.

Once upon a time, a time that ran from the seventeenth century
into the second half of the twentieth century, the *who* of theology, the
description of those who did theology, could be stated very simply: theology in the Catholic Church was the preserve of ordained ministers.
This simple answer to the *who* also determined the *where, what,* and
how: theology was studied primarily in seminaries; it was the means by
which men were equipped with all the knowledge necessary for a minister in the church of that time; and it was done principally by learning
how the great figures in the history of the church and the church's official teachers had sought to explain various aspects of God and God's
relationship to humanity.

The *who* and the *where* of theology as described above were
largely responsible for the perception that theology was something
recondite, something to be left to specialists who were male and

ordained. Theology was not for the ordinary members of the church. Theology reached the nonordained members of the church only via their bishops and priests. In this context, theology was largely about directions for how life was to be lived in a godly way. These directions had been formulated in the past, and the present task was simply to follow them.

At the end of the twentieth century, however, the situation for theology is much changed. Theology is still studied by candidates for ordination, but these seminarians often share their classes with other students—women and men; single, married, widowed, and divorced—who are not candidates for ordination. Indeed, seminarians can be the minority group in these classes. In addition, seminaries are no longer the sole venue, for courses in theology can be pursued not only at some universities, where theology has been available for many years, but also in parishes and even in schools. So changed is the *who* of theology that at least one "how to" guide stresses that people of different colors, nationalities, ages, genders, educational backgrounds, talents, and handicaps must find for themselves a theology that represents them adequately.[1] In short, the *who* of theology has become all-inclusive. Accordingly, while this book is directed primarily to those undertaking formal studies in theology, its content will also be relevant to all members of the church who desire to deepen, through the study of theology, both their understanding of their faith and their active life as Christians.

The radical change in the *who* of theology has been accompanied by an equally significant shift in the *how* and the *what* of theology. Theology is now less associated with answers and directives handed on from the past as a closed body of knowledge; it is now more concerned with activity, with the search to discern how to express the meaning of faith and how to respond to God in the present. As we will see, this search does not require a repudiation of the past, but it does require that there be a dialogue between the past and the present, a dialogue that was often neglected in the history of theology.

For the first half of the twentieth century, Catholic theology was dominated by the various schools of commentary on the theology of St. Thomas Aquinas. Today, however, there are almost as many ways to do theology as there are people who do it. Indeed, the study of *theological method,* the manner in which one does theology, has itself become a major field of interest for theologians. Not surprisingly, this development has meant that the content of theology is no longer dominated by issues that are relevant principally to those preparing for ordained ministry. The fact that contemporary theology is concerned with issues such as economics and the environment reflects the broader base from which theologians themselves are drawn nowadays.

Thus far, we have painted a picture of theology as a discipline that has undergone major developments in recent decades, as a vibrant activity undertaken today by many people in many different ways. What has not been addressed explicitly, however, is what all these people are doing. In other words, what is theology?

In order to move toward an answer, we will analyze a number of different definitions drawn from readily available introductory studies of theology. These definitions will not only provide some insight into what theology is, but will also help to set the agenda for the remainder of this chapter and the remainder of this book.

What Is Theology?

The first definition is rather stark:

Theology may be defined as the study which, through participation in and reflection upon a religious faith, seeks to express the content of this faith in the clearest and most coherent language available.[2]

This definition offers us five important themes. First, it declares that theology proceeds from "religious faith." In other words, theology is not simply the study of religion, but it is the study of religion from the perspective of faith. This means that the theologian, unlike the practitioner of religious studies, does not stand outside the particular religion in order to examine its origins, beliefs, and structures as a disinterested observer: the theologian is an "insider," someone whose own life is shaped by faith.

Second, the definition takes for granted that the religious faith on which theology reflects has content, that it is neither illusion nor delusion. If this is true, then it follows that an appreciation of theology is dependent on an understanding of the term *faith* and, in particular, an understanding of what is meant by "the content of this faith." This exploration of faith will also require us to investigate what it means to claim that our faith is a response to revelation, to God's self-communication. In addition, it will be important to explore whether, as is often asserted, faith is at odds with reason, whether faith necessitates the sacrifice of our capacity for critical thinking (issues that will be addressed in chapter 3).

Third, the definition is underpinned by the conviction that theology, because it is a manifestation of the capacity for reflection and for the use of language and symbol, is unequivocally a human activity. If we are to establish the legitimacy of a theology that builds on such foundations, we need to examine the legitimacy of the foundations themselves. In other words, we must investigate whether the capacity for reflection and the use of language and symbols are indeed fundamental to what it means to be human (the concern of chapter 2). Similarly, we need to explore some of the mechanisms that human beings use to reflect on their experience; that is, we need to delve into the role philosophy plays in theology (as we will do in chapter 5).

Fourth, the definition makes us aware that theology, precisely because it is about "religious faith," is not the exclusive preserve of any one religion. Thus, the followers of Islam, Judaism, and the world's other religions have developed theologies that express the content of their particular faith. While acknowledging that theology is not the prerogative of any one group, this book is an exercise in *Christian* theology; that is, it focuses on the experience and the theology of Christians, people who build their lives on faith in the God who has been mediated to human beings through Jesus Christ.

Fifth, the definition alerts us to the fact that theology is done by people who bring their personal faith into dialogue with an already-existing tradition of faith. In other words, theology is never *creatio ex nihilo* (creation from nothing), but it involves the interpretation of "the content of this faith" which predates all of us. It will be a primary concern of this chapter to discuss what there is to interpret and what makes interpretation necessary.

As useful as our first definition is, it is not the only possible definition, a fact that is not surprising since theology involves, as we have just indicated, two multifaceted realities: God and human beings. The next definition can therefore be expected to advance our search for an understanding of theology:

> *Theology is concerned with our experience of God, particularly our experience of God as a community of faith. It is the effort to*

understand and interpret the faith experience of a community, to bring it to expression in language and symbol.[3]

The nub of this description is its emphasis on the fact that theology issues from a community's, not merely an individual's, experience of God—an idea flagged already as the fifth point of our original definition. This emphasis does not deny the individual's experience, but it implies that individual experience is understood best when it is brought into relationship with the experience of a group. Even though, as we shall see in chapter 4, it is certainly true that the notion of "the people" is central to the Bible, the emphasis on the value of a group is not an exclusively religious insight. Indeed, much contemporary sociology and psychology share the conviction, which will be discussed further in the next chapter, that we are most fully ourselves when we are in relationship with others.

The emphasis on the value of the community implies that if we promote individual experience as the measure of all things, we circumscribe our possibilities for development. In other words, as the history of science illustrates well, if we were to deny ourselves the knowledge and insight that can be provided by the experience of others, our possibilities for growth would be restricted to the insights we might discover in the course of a single lifetime. The likelihood of a growth in insight increases significantly when we draw from the wisdom of others, not only of our contemporaries, but also of our forebears, whose wisdom can still speak to us despite the fact that the circumstances of their lives were different from ours.

It is equally true, however, as the history of human enterprises as diverse as the arts and sport clearly reveals, that the group can reject the experience of the individual when his or her experience challenges the prevailing values and approach of the group. In other words, the group, because of a reluctance to embrace any changes, can set its face against the enrichment that might be provided to it by the experience and insight of its gifted individual members. Such intransigence is, of course, no less toxic than unrestrained individualism.

From the two definitions we have examined thus far, we have learned that theology reflects on the human experience—individual and communal—of God, and that it articulates that experience in words and symbols. The next definition will take us one step further:

Theology today may be understood as a discipline which seeks to understand and determine the underlying truth of all reality. Christian theology does not merely talk about God. Rather theology attempts to construe all things, the world, human existence, human history and society, as well as God from within the vision that is mediated to the Christian community by its religious symbols.[4]

This definition challenges the idea that theology, while it is certainly about God and religious faith, is concerned solely with what is "religious," where that word implies a narrow world of cult or doctrine. On the contrary, theology is about "all things," for only such a focus can do justice both to the God whom we believe is the source of all things and to human beings, the practitioners of theology, who are involved in "all things."

If it is to do justice to the God present in all things, theology needs to be inclusive; it needs to identify where God is present in all things. This principle is illustrated well in the theology of Karl Rahner (1904–84), one of the most significant Catholic theologians in the history of the church. Rahner is renowned for his insights into the meaning of the Trinity and other profound aspects of the relationship between God and humanity, but he also published a series of theological reflections on such seemingly nontheological topics as sitting down, eating, laughter, and sleep.[5]

The fact that God can be discussed in relation to any human experience provides an appropriate connection to a theme that the last two definitions have mentioned: theology's relationship to symbols. Theology expresses, by means of a reasoned explanation, the faith of the community that is symbolized in the liturgy, in doctrine, in art, or in music. In so doing, theological discourse can itself symbolize the faith of the community.

The first goal that any discussion of symbols must accomplish is to overcome the popular, but false, perception that "the symbol" is equivalent to "the unreal"—a perception reflected in comments such as "It's *just* a symbol." It is ironic that symbols are so regarded when, in fact, it is possible to argue that reality can be apprehended *only* via symbols. Unlike what we might more easily accept as "real," symbols have a depth of meaning that is not exhausted by what we see. Symbols convey, through what is seen, a level of meaning and reality that always remains unseen, but that is nonetheless present. Symbols remind us of the complexity of reality; they remind us that reality is not one-dimensional and transparent, and that not every aspect of human experience can be exhausted by one short sentence. In fact, we use symbols as short-hand to convey complexity and richness. An example of a symbol used in business, sport, politics, the arts, and most other fields of human endeavor is the figure of the hero. When heroes in any of those fields are held up to us, we know that they are not simply Person X, but that their deeds and words communicate such invisible characteristics as courage, loyalty, wisdom, perseverance, and generosity.

Symbols, because they enable us to communicate in a concrete and accessible way the most profound and multifaceted truths, have always played an important role in the articulation and celebration of Christianity. In the context of the Christian faith, the fundamental symbol is Jesus himself: Jesus who exists in history as a fully human being; Jesus who is also, at the same time and in the same appearance, *Emmanuel,* God-with-us. The Christian claim makes Jesus the perfect symbol, because in him is expressed entirely the unseen reality of God and the full potential of our humanity. It is one of the tasks of theology, of the particular branch of theology called Christology, to elucidate the symbolic reality of Jesus. Such theology emerges out of—that is, it is subsequent to and dependent on—the community's faith that Jesus Christ is truly the symbol of God.

The church's response to God is expressed in the symbols used in the communal liturgy, in creeds, and in hymns and other prayers. Even though the community's faith in, and response to, God's revelation in Jesus Christ precede the effort to express their meaning through the reflective processes of theology, they do not make this effort irrelevant. Indeed, theology provides the members of the church with the concepts and words that enable them not only to grow in understanding of their own faith, but also to speak to others of their faith. In other words, theology can itself symbolize the faith of the community.

Our final description of theology emphasizes that theology cannot be restricted to providing information about God, but is also the source of critical reflection on how the community lives its faith:

> *Theology is reflection, a critical attitude. Theology follows; it is the second step. What Hegel used to say about philosophy can likewise be applied to theology: it rises only at sundown. The pastoral activity of the Church does not flow as a conclusion from*

*theological premises. Theology does not produce pastoral activ-
ity; rather it reflects upon it. Theology must be able to find in pastoral activity the presence of the Spirit inspiring the action of the
Christian community.*[6]

This description highlights that if theology's subject matter is not
exclusively what is "religious," if theology is about life, the test of a
theology's value is whether it connects us better with life. In other
words, theology challenges the Christian community, in the name of
Jesus who calls us to a discipleship that involves a deeper engagement
with the world and its people who are loved by God, to live in such a
way that it offers hope to the world and its people. Theology, as we will
discuss in detail in chapters 6 and 7, does not aim merely to provide
more information about either God or human existence; rather, it con-
fronts us with the radical vision for life that is at the heart of the gospel.

Our examination of the four previous definitions or descriptions
of theology may have produced the impression that theology is too
complex to be pursued. As was indicated in the introduction, however,
the complexity of theology reflects the paradox that we human beings
find it difficult to comprehend the mystery of God's simplicity. In addition, it reflects the fact that because we human beings share in the mystery of God, we too cannot be reduced to a few simple notions.
Theology is complex, therefore, because in dealing with God and ourselves it seeks to be all-inclusive: theology excludes no human experience from its ambit, for it is in these experiences that God is present.

Each of the four definitions stresses that theology is an activity—
thus, we can speak of "doing theology"—and not simply a body of
knowledge to be learned. But is there one word that can encapsulate the
nature of that activity? Candidates for the role of this key word would
be *interpretation, mediation,* and *translation.* These words share the
sense of standing between two distinct but related periods or groups;
they highlight the fact that theology provides a connection between the
past and the present, between the faith of those who have taught us
about God and our faith in God in the present.

Theology presumes that these two "ages" of faith are related but
also distinct. It presumes too that we in the present do not simply repeat
the past, even in terms of our awareness of God, and that the past is not so
alien to us that it cannot speak to us in any way. It is both the differences
and connection between the past and the present that make necessary the

mediation, interpretation, and translation that are the work of theology. Thus, the differences between our forebears and ourselves, between their use of concepts and language and the concepts and language that are congenial to us today, make interpretation, translation, and mediation necessary, but not impossible. A theology that mediates between the past and the present is possible because we share with our forebears such things as a corporeal and social existence, a relationship with the physical environment, and a quest for meaning in our lives.[7]

The past that is to be mediated to the present has a particular resonance in theology. It refers not simply to what predates our own time, but (as was indicated in some of the definitions) to the preexisting faith of the Christian community, the church. Our next task is therefore to explore the relationship between theology and the church. This will be a rich field of exploration because it will require that we address the relationship between the individual believer and the church not only as a general question, but also in its more specific forms: namely, the role that Scripture, tradition, and the church's teaching authority play in the business of "doing theology."

Theology and the Church

When we speak today of *God* or *Jesus Christ,* we know that we are not the originators of either these words or what they imply; in fact, we know that Christians have used these words for two millennia. More specifically, we know that even the ways in which we use these words today have been shaped by the insights of those who lived before us. Although it is crucial for the treatment of theology in this book to emphasize that no ages, communities, or individuals have ever responded to God in the same way that we—in our age, in our present-day communities, or as individuals—respond to God, this fact does not gainsay another truth: we are dependent on those who have spoken about God before us. This means that our experience of God has to be brought into dialogue with existing expressions of faith.

In this democratic age, we might want to insist that we are as entitled as our forebears to determine what can be said about God. We might want to assert that we could come up with a much better idea of God than they did, that we could produce a deity who is both less complex and more accessible than God often seems to be in traditional

Christianity. Such a god, however, would not be the God of Jesus Christ, since the God of Jesus Christ can be named only through the ideas and language that come to us from the history of faith.

The God whom Jesus called *abba* (Mk 14:36) was not an *a priori* concept, not a God designed by a think tank, but a God who chose to be known explicitly at a certain time and in a certain culture, with all the limits of that time and culture. This does not mean that human knowledge and understanding of God can never develop beyond the articulation that occurred in the century after the death of Jesus—indeed, it is a central purpose of this chapter to emphasize that we must articulate today a contemporary understanding of God—but it does certainly mean that Christians in every age are dependent on those who experienced directly the life and message of Jesus. We are dependent on them because only their witness can help us to identify our experience as an experience of the Spirit of Jesus.

This fact may be discouraging, not only because it means that we, people who live in the age of the modem and the satellite telephone, are dependent on what we have received from a pretechnological people, but also because it means we cannot avoid the church.

The prominence given to the church in this section might disappoint those who either are committed to unfettered individualism or fear that the excesses in the church's history of authority inevitably mean that the insights of the individual believer will be suppressed in favor of the interests of the group. Since a large section of what remains to be discussed in this chapter builds on the claim that the role of the church is essential, it is important that we address immediately the objections to the church that arise both from the philosophy of individualism and from the church's own history.

The first task is to establish why the church as a whole, rather than simply individual believers, is essential to theology. Put simply, the church is essential to the process of theology because it is the church that has preserved the witness to Jesus. The church has preserved this witness because it is the foundation of the church's own existence. Indeed, as the Second Vatican Council expressed it, the church was formed and shaped by the Spirit of Jesus to be the body that kept alive in the world the good news of God's kingdom, which was preached by Jesus himself.[8] Dependence on the church gives us, therefore, an access to Jesus that none of us could achieve through our individual resources.

It is certainly true that each of us has a unique experience of Jesus, an experience that can enrich every member of the church, but it is equally true that our membership in the church can benefit us immeasurably because it unites us with an experience of Jesus that extends across time and culture, an experience none of us could achieve in the space of our one lifetime. In other words, dependence on the church liberates us from the limits of individualism. The implications for theology of this principle are best seen in the fact that both the scriptures and tradition are fundamental to the process of theology.

Theology and the Church: The Bible

There is a temptation to think of the Bible as a magical book, independent of any history or authorial details and certainly independent of the church. In fact, the Bible is perceived correctly only when it is recognized that it is the church's book.

The phrase "the church's book" might not sit comfortably with us. It could suggest that the church asserts proprietary rights over the book, such as the right to determine who can have access to it. The claim that the Bible is the church's book is not, however, an attempt by the church to usurp the authority of scripture, but is the recognition that the scriptures as we now know them were not only gathered together by a decision of the church, but are given their unique status and authority in the church because they continue to mediate to the members of the church an experience of Jesus as the unsurpassable revelation of God. The scriptures remain for the church the primary means of access to God's revelation in Jesus.

The scriptures function, therefore, as a norm for the church's faith. As we shall see in chapter 4, this does not mean that theology is able only to offer commentaries on the Bible; it does not mean that every passage of scripture has a meaning that is always obvious or that every passage of scripture has an equal importance. It does mean, however, that taken as a whole, the scriptures function as a negative norm for theology within the church.[9] In other words, the church would not accept from any individual theologian or group within the church a portrayal of God, an analysis of Jesus, or an interpretation of Christian discipleship that contradicted explicitly either what the Bible might say on those topics or the church's interpretation of the Bible's portrayal of God. Clearly, this statement raises a variety of issues about who makes such decisions and with what criteria. But the key point to note is that the church has never considered itself free to go against the scriptures, because they express its own foundations, its link to those who witnessed to the death and resurrection of Jesus and the ongoing presence of the Spirit. The scriptures are the principal reminder to us that the church is a community of faith that we are not free to remake in our own image.

It is in this context of the need to preserve our connection to Jesus that we can begin to discuss the role of tradition both in the life of the church in general and in theology in particular.

Theology and the Church: Tradition

Many people in the church are suspicious of "tradition" because it has often been invoked to justify opposition to anything new in theology and in the life of the church. For this reason, it might be feared that the introduction of tradition to illustrate the importance of the church's relationship to theology is a ruse designed to stifle creativity in theology. In order to appropriate tradition positively, we must recognize immediately that it is wrong to regard tradition, as it was often suggested in the dispute between Catholics and Protestants that followed the Reformation, as a body of knowledge that is not contained in the Bible but that is nonetheless known to the church.

While it is notoriously difficult to define tradition precisely, we gain our best insight into tradition if we associate it primarily with the dynamic nature of the church's faith, and especially with what enables the church to live this faith in a world of change, rather than with nonscriptural knowledge that is available to the church. The task of the church—and indeed of theology—in a changing world is twofold: to maintain its links to its origins and to develop its faith in response to new situations. Tradition aids the fulfillment of this twofold task. This means that tradition can be grasped fully only if it is associated both with the handing on of the church's faith, which is expressed in the scriptures and the creeds, and with the Spirit who animates the church's faith.

Tradition relates to the lived faith of the members of the church, the faith that enables them, through the guidance of the Spirit, to recognize the presence of God. In other words, tradition in its fullest sense does not refer simply to the knowledge that exists in the Church, but to

the Spirit alive in the church. The Spirit who was at work in the formation of both the scriptures and the doctrines of the church is also at
work in the members of the church who today read the scriptures, study
the church's doctrines, and listen to the questions of our time in order to
discern how we are to respond to God in the present. That Spirit is at
work in the present to achieve the same aims that it has always sought
to achieve: to enable the members of the church not only to hold fast to
what connects them to Jesus but also to move in new directions that are
faithful to the revelation of God in Jesus.

The presence of the Spirit, which constitutes the tradition of the
church, enables the church to do more than simply repeat the past: the
Spirit gives the church the confidence to believe that it does not simply
have to choose between either the preservation of the past or a response
to the present. The Spirit gives the church the confidence to believe that
its faith in Jesus can always grow deeper and that the expression of this
faith is capable of endless development because there will always be
more to the revelation of God in Jesus than the church has grasped and
expressed at any one point of its history.

In all of this, the presumption is not only that the Spirit is at work
to ensure that the church, as it strives to respond to the new challenges
of its history, does not lose its connection to Jesus, but also that the
Spirit is present for the good of the whole church and not simply for
any one member or group of members. In other words, our relationship
with the church—a relationship that begins in baptism and is nurtured
through the scriptures, the sacraments, the teachings of the church, and
the faith of those with whom we share our membership in the church—
gives us access to what none of us could achieve by our own efforts.

The Spirit does not give the church a blueprint to follow, but, as
Vatican II recognized in its document on revelation, it works through the
contemplation and study of believers who ponder truth in their hearts,
through their intimate understanding of what is spiritual, and through
the work of the bishops who exercise "the sure charism of truth."[10]

This reference to the bishops' role in the determination of what is
a valid expression of the church's faith returns us to what we identified
as the possible second objection to the assertion that there is an intimate
connection between theology and the church: the fear that the church's
teaching authority has been so compromised by its use—or abuse—of

authority that it can no longer legitimately claim that it has a central role to play in the processes of theology.

Theology and the Church: The Teaching Authority

The exercise of authority in the church arouses strong emotions. Whereas some members of the church promote the need for an authority that is vigorous and absolute because it alone can prevent Catholics from sliding into the mire of individualism and loss of identity, other members of the church see authority as too restrictive, too male, and too little committed to dialogue and openness. The fact that there is such a polarized view of authority in the church makes it urgent not only that we clarify the relationship between theology and the teaching authority, but that in order to avoid the issue being seen simply as a dispute about who has power, we situate that relationship within the context of the church and its mission.

The first point to stress is that the church is not composed of an omniscient teaching authority—often referred to as the *magisterium,* a name derived from the Latin word for those whose special competence in a field qualified them to be teachers—and a mass of ignorant members. Indeed, as the Second Vatican Council affirmed, it is the whole body of the faithful, anointed by the Spirit, that is infallible in matters of faith.[11] This means that the authority of the bishops and the pope is related to, and cannot be substituted for, the faith of the whole church. What, then, is the relationship of the authoritative teaching body and the rest of the church?

Perhaps the best answer to this question is to say that the teaching authority or magisterium has ultimate responsibility for the unity of the church's faith. That answer might lead to a further question: why is there a need for anyone to exercise such a responsibility? A response to this new question will be possible only when we have reflected briefly on the purpose of the church's existence.

If, as Christians believe—and as will be discussed more fully in chapter 3—Jesus is God's unsurpassable self-revelation, and if that revelation is for all people, then it must be possible for all people to have access to it. The church is the means of that access. This, in turn, implies that the church, the community of those who center their lives on Jesus Christ, must have a clear expression of its faith, a means to preserve its unity, to maintain its identity, and to resolve internal conflicts.[12] If the church lacked all such mechanisms, and if the church continually changed its shape and self-definition, it could hardly maintain that it represented God's definitive self-revelation.

The existence of the bishops as an authoritative teaching body, therefore, cannot be separated from the church's existence in history. The teaching authority exists to be "responsible for the emergence of the right relation between the community of believers and the content of faith which is prior to it, and is responsible for ensuring proper communication within the Church."[13] The teaching authority, therefore, is a tangible reminder to us that the faith we share as members of the church is a faith that is dependent on those who have preserved the meaning of God's revelation in Jesus Christ and passed it on to us. In other words, the existence of the teaching authority reinforces the fact that our church is founded in history, that it cannot be remade for every new age, and that it is not the home of unrestrained individualism. We contribute to the well-being of the church, therefore, when we develop and maintain a positive relationship to the church's teaching office. Such a positive relationship is not possible without an awareness of both the different types of teaching that can come from the pope and bishops and the different types of assent that those teachings call for from all the members of the church.[14]

Although the teaching authority is a guard against the church's loss of identity and purpose, it is not designed to be a bulwark against history or change. Indeed, we could argue that if there were no possibility of change in the church, there would be no need for an authority to preside over the preservation of identity in the midst of change. Equally, while theologians promote development of the church's faith, they are not advocates of ending the continuity of the church's faith. Rather, the teaching authority and the theologians ought to be united in the essential task of theology: to translate the church's tradition of faith for a new context.

The fact that the mission of theologians and that of the teaching authority can be linked in this way means that we need to say something about the particular relationship between the teaching authority and theology. The teaching authority is certainly not the only body in the Catholic Church that does theology, it is not the catalyst or source for every effort to do theology in the church, and it is not a body whose permission must be sought before any of us can either undertake courses in theology or develop our own theology on any topic. Like an umpire in a sporting event, the teaching authority is the body that is ultimately responsible for the maintenance of unity in the church. More specifically, it is the body that has the right to determine what in theology is or is not faithful to the tradition of the church. We may dispute the manner in which the teaching authority carries out its function, we may wish to see it act with a more pronounced spirit of justice and sensitivity, but even these criticisms of its practice can recognize that the function of the teaching authority is a vital one for the well-being of the church and its mission in the world. The significant role that the teaching authority has in regard to theology makes it essential that bishops and theologians continue to speak with one another in order to refine the dynamics of their relationship.

The fact that we can identify a need for the teaching authority and theologians to develop a more positive relationship demonstrates that the history of that relationship has been a checkered one. The exercise of authority in the church has not always been consistent with the demands of truth, justice, or charity, just as the practice of theologians has not always reflected their responsibility to the whole church. A clear understanding of the respective contributions that the teaching authority and theologians can make to the well-being of the church allows us to challenge either party—and both parties—when they fail to exhibit a life-giving approach to what is ultimately a shared mission.

Now that we have explored the essential elements that make up theology in the Catholic tradition, our next task is to examine how these elements operate together. We will do this by reviewing some of the different methods that have been used, or are being used today, to do theology in the Catholic tradition.

"Doing Theology" in the Past and the Present

The history of theology illustrates amply that theology is susceptible to a seemingly limitless variety of approaches or methods. Theologians in every age have been adept at the work of interpretation, the work of expressing the church's heritage of faith in new ways. At times the specific aim of this interpretation has been to refute objections to faith raised by non-Christian thinkers, and at other times it has been to identify how Christians might live as disciples of Jesus in circumstances far removed from those of Jesus himself. In addition, the history of theology shows us clearly that there is no single language or philosophy that must be used as the vehicle for our talk about God: theologians throughout history have "baptized" many forms of thought and conscripted many styles of expression to aid their work of interpretation.

In the century after the death of Jesus, Christianity moved from being a faith preserved by oral tradition within communities to a faith with a series of written texts that were gradually accepted as the normative expression of the community's experience of Jesus. It is important to realize, however, that even those texts that we know collectively as the New Testament reflect a variety of emphases and styles, which express not merely the individual genius of their authors but also the situation and needs of their original readership. In other words, the New Testament is not only a reference text for theologians, but it is itself theology or, more accurately, theologies. Thus, we find in the Gospels not one portrayal of Jesus, but four different portrayals that attempt to clarify the experience of God's revelation in Jesus and to identify how the faithful might respond to that revelation.

Although the formation of the New Testament gave the Christian community a definitive text that it could use in its liturgies and that remains the normative expression of its experience of Jesus, its formation certainly did not mean the end of theology. In fact, the New Testament itself became the stimulus for further theology, because its very existence raised issues such as how to interpret texts and how to express in a fuller form the community's faith that the Jesus of the Gospels was the revelation of God. In addition, the first generations of Christians had to articulate their faith in a context that increasingly required that they not only distinguish Christianity from Judaism, but also that they respond to the worldview of those who were formed in the wisdom of Greek philosophy.

To fulfill these various tasks, Christian thinkers drew at different times on the religious imagery of Judaism and the philosophical forms and vocabulary of the Greeks. Since Jesus had not supplied his followers with a privileged language and conceptual framework that they could use when they referred to him, they expressed their experience and understanding in the frameworks that their culture made available to them.

Thus from its beginnings, Christian theology was multidimensional and pluralist. As mentioned above, the four Gospels and the Pauline writings cannot be reduced to one all-encompassing version of the life of Jesus; nor can the competing theologies that emerged from the "schools" of Alexandria and Antioch and that were influenced by Aristotelian and Platonic concepts respectively be reduced to a single theological method. This is a vital point, for it indicates that we ought not to expect that theology can be done today in just one way. Interpretation can, therefore, be manifold without necessarily being destructive of the unity of the church's faith. The church itself recognized from its earliest days that it needed a mechanism to determine when the diversity of expressions and emphases was destructive. From this need emerged the notion of councils as a concrete way to signify the Spirit's guidance that enabled the church to maintain its unity in faith.

As the church developed, so too did its theological history. By the end of the first millennium, not only were there creeds that could be used to summarize the faith of the church, but there also was a vast amount of reflection on the meaning of faith in Jesus Christ, reflection that dealt not only with doctrinal issues but also with numerous issues of liturgy, spirituality, and individual and social behavior. In addition to these internal stimuli to the church's theological development, the society of which the church was a part continued to provide stimuli for developments in theology. Nothing illustrates that better than the revival in Aristotelian studies during the twelfth century in Europe.

The introduction of Aristotle, a philosopher who lived four centuries before Jesus Christ, challenged many of the assumptions on which theology had relied for centuries. The vitality of thought that found its inspiration in Aristotle also highlighted the fact that much of Christian philosophy had become pedestrian during the long centuries when the Christian worldview dominated Western Europe. Aristotle's thought, particularly his stress on the empirical basis of all human knowledge, necessitated a thorough review of the premises on which theology operated. This rethinking and the development of a new approach to theology were accomplished principally by Thomas Aquinas (1225–74), who was able to incorporate the insights of Aristotelian philosophy into his approach to grace, God's presence in our lives.[15]

Following the Renaissance, the next major challenge to theology came from the Protestant Reformation. The Catholic Church's response, articulated largely by the Council of Trent (1545–63), stressed its differences from Protestantism. For most of the period from the sixteenth century until the middle years of the twentieth century, Catholic theology continued to be influenced primarily by the work of Thomas Aquinas or, more accurately, by the style of theology known as Scholasticism, which was based on Thomas but lacked his creativity. In addition, Catholic theology strenuously resisted the new ideas that emerged especially in the eighteenth and nineteenth centuries as a result of the Enlightenment and industrialization in Europe.

It would be accurate to describe these as very lean centuries for theology in the Catholic Church, as centuries when the church seemed to be desperately afraid of the world and unable to respond to the ideas of people such as Karl Marx, Friedrich Nietzsche, or Sigmund Freud. Sadly, not only was there a noticeable dearth of the creativity that had been evident for much of the history of theology, but also those in authority in the church were particularly unresponsive to new ideas. Since the middle years of the twentieth century, however, that situation has altered markedly.

The single greatest stimulus to the renewal—perhaps "explosion" is not an overstatement—of theology that has occurred since the middle years of the twentieth century was the Second Vatican Council. The Council recognized that the gospel could be proclaimed effectively only if the church sought a more fruitful relationship with the world to which it belongs. The Council also recognized that this goal required the church to review all aspects of its life, from its liturgy to its understanding of the human dynamics of marriage.

The work of the Council, however, did not occur in a vacuum. It was able to achieve as much as it did because the way had been prepared by the efforts of theologians such as Karl Rahner, Henri de Lubac, Yves Congar, and John Courtney Murray, all of whom had been regarded with suspicion during theology's lean years immediately after World War II. These theologians emphasized the need to return to the church's heritage of faith—a process the French theologians called *ressourcement*—and to recover from that heritage treasures that had been left undeveloped. These treasures provided the basis for a dialogue with questions of the modern world, questions that could not be addressed merely by a repetition of the theological formulas of the post-Reformation world. In addition, theologians such as Rahner and

Bernard Lonergan sought to bring Christian faith into dialogue with contemporary philosophy in much the same way as Thomas had brought it into dialogue with Aristotle.

Vatican II summoned the church to a dialogue with the wisdom of the modern world. In order to participate in such a dialogue, the church itself needed to recover its own dynamism, its own capacity for development. In other words, the church needed to rediscover that the life of the Spirit within it meant that the church had nothing to fear from that openness to the world that Pope John XXIII promoted as the process of *aggiornamento* or renewal. The work of the theologians discussed above contributed greatly to this renewal. They identified for the church the resources it could use to address the questions of the modern world. Their work provides a powerful example of how theology can fulfill its role of translation, mediation, and interpretation of the church's tradition for a new situation.

Catholic theology in the generation since Vatican II has been more multifaceted and pluralistic than at any previous time in its history. Today the practitioners of liberation theology have not only placed the poor at the center of the theological enterprise, but they have also stressed that theology cannot separate itself from the insights that social analysis can provide. The liberation theologians have highlighted for the church the crucial connection that must exist between theology and *praxis* or action. This connection, which saves theology from degenerating into a "head trip," will be investigated more thoroughly in the final chapter of this book. Another major development has been the rise of feminist theology, which is itself an expression of liberation theology. Feminist theologians have emphasized the unique perspective that comes from the experience of women, an experience that for too long was ignored within the Catholic tradition.

The emergence of both liberation and feminist theologies attests to the vitality of the Christian faith. That both theologies have been met with some suspicion within the Christian community reminds us that the church, particularly as represented by its teaching authority, has as a primary—and positive—task the conservation of the faith that has been inherited. This commitment to conservation might make us wary of what is new, but it should not be equated with a refusal to accept that the tradition can also develop. This means that liberation and feminist theologies need to be approached from a perspective that recognizes that Christian theologians will always seek to express the truth of the tradition in new ways in response to social and cultural changes.

This principle is also illustrated in the work of those theologians who are seeking to interpret the Christian message in the context of postmodern philosophies, the emergence of quantum physics, the ecological movement, economic rationalism, and the breathtaking developments in technology and communications. In addition, theology has also broken out of its denominational shackles as Christian theologians from different ecclesial traditions seek to express their common heritage of faith and enter together into dialogue with non-Christians.

This portrayal of the dynamism of theology is clearly a long way from the settled and closely ordered period that followed the Council of Trent. Understandably, that shift has come about too quickly and too dramatically for many in the church. Although we must marvel at the breadth of the change, we can also recognize that it has not been without its difficulties. Principal among these difficulties has been the breakdown of the notion that theology is an ecclesial enterprise in which the teaching authority has a legitimate and important role to play. This breakdown is not difficult to understand in the light of the history of the last hundred years, in which the teaching authority was often repressive, but for anyone who subscribes to the notion that theology is inextricably linked to the community of faith, the breakdown is nonetheless a distressing development that only the conversion of all parties can heal.

The reference to conversion in the previous paragraph can serve as a bridge to the final concern of this chapter: the connection between theology and spirituality. This is a significant issue because it reinforces the claim that theology is not simply an intellectual pursuit.

Theology and Spirituality

The commitment to theology requires a spiritual effort to grow in virtue and holiness.[16]

We might wonder why anyone would advance the claim that involvement with theology must affect the life of its practitioners in such a significant way. We might wonder whether the same requirement would be mandatory for the person who works as a pathologist, a bank teller, or a taxi driver. What is at issue here is not simply the expectation that the theologian ought to be honest and assiduous, because we would surely expect all people to exhibit these virtues in their business or professional undertakings. What is at issue is the relationship between the subject matter of theology and the practitioner of theology. The quote implies that the person who, according to the principle that has shaped this chapter, seeks to bring the tradition of faith into dialogue with the present, the person who spends time "looking into the sun," as Karl Barth (1886–1968), arguably the most influential Protestant theologian of the twentieth century, described the occupation of the theologian, cannot remain unaffected by this occupation, cannot but desire to grow in virtue and holiness.[17] Can such an assertion be justified?

In order to answer this question, we need to return to an idea discussed earlier: that theology proceeds from faith in a loving God who is present in all things. If theologians are dealing intimately with this truth, if they are guiding others in their desire to recognize and respond to such a God, it follows that theologians cannot demand immunity when their own insights into the meaning of a faithful response to this God promote the need for a reform of attitudes or actions. Thus, although we can imagine that the pathologist, the bank teller, and the taxi driver have aspects of their lives on which viruses, customers, and passengers respectively impinge not at all, theologians, if they are truly concerned with the God present in "all things," if they want to live with no disjunction between their words and their own lives, cannot be detached from their "work."

None of this means that only people with obsessive personalities make good theologians or good students of theology. None of this means that theologians are unable to relax, unable to talk at parties about anything other than God. Nor does it mean that theologians are always people of lustrous virtue, exorbitantly gifted individuals who tower above the common herd to which their contemporaries are consigned. Theologians ought to be, however, people who are aware in all things, including even the conversation at parties, of the God of infinite love.

Theologians ought to be aware that our response to the God of infinite love will often call us to let go of those things in our lives that do not reflect this God. In other words, theologians and students of theology, no less than any other members of the Christian community, ought to be attuned to the fact that our involvement with the living God will confront us with the need for conversion: the need to open, and even to change, our minds, our affections, and our actions in response to God.

The theologian is not a virtuoso before whom the other members of the community of faith can only stand spellbound; the theologian is a resource for all the members of the community of faith as they attempt to respond to God in the present in a way that is faithful to the community's tradition. In order to be an authentic resource for the community, the theologian must not only be steeped in the tradition and aware of the exigencies of the present, but the theologian must also, above all, be a person who is open to God:

> *The foundation [of theology] is not a set of objective statements but rather the subjective reality of the persons who reflect upon their religious experience, and especially on the basic process we call conversion.*[18]

This means that it is essential for theologians to nurture their own life of faith. Unless this happens, there is a danger that theologians will focus on their own wisdom rather than God's. By contrast, prayer involves us in the recognition of our incompleteness before God.[19] Such a recognition saves us both from making idols of ourselves and from believing that only our own insights are worthwhile. A theology that aims to nurture the Christian community must avoid such dangers. Unless theologians find their strength and inspiration in the life of the Spirit, there is not only the possibility that their theology will recognize no standard other than their own insights, but there is also the possibility that their theology will cease to exercise a properly critical and prophetic function in regard to the church's response to Jesus Christ. If this happens, then theology ceases to be of service to the church. What must be nurtured by theologians, therefore, is their own relationship to God as members of the Christian community:

> *Contemplation, far from being opposed to theology, is in fact the normal perfection of theology. We must not separate intellectual study of divinely revealed truth and contemplative experience of that truth as if they could never have anything to do with one another. On the contrary, they are simply two aspects of the same thing. Dogmatic and mystical theology, or theology and "spirituality" are not to be set apart in mutually exclusive categories.... [The] two belong together just as body and soul belong together. Unless they are united, there is no fervor, no life and no spiritual value in theology, no meaning, no sure orientation in the contemplative life.*[20]

The hope that underpins this book is that the study of theology will be the means not just for intellectual growth, but also for a renewed awareness of the God who is present in all things and who calls each of us, individually and as a community of faith, to live as disciples of Jesus Christ in the world.

QUESTIONS FOR REFLECTION

1. Why is it valid to argue that theology is more than an intellectual exercise?

2. Is it accurate to refer to the church as the "home" of theology?

3. What are the major social and cultural influences on contemporary theology?

4. What is the connection between theology and Christian discipleship?

SUGGESTIONS FOR FURTHER READING

- Geffré, Claude and Werner Jeanrond, eds. *Why Theology? Concilium* (1994).

- O'Donovan, Leo J. and T. Howland Sanks, eds. *Faithful Witness: Foundations of Theology for Today's Church.* New York: Crossroad, 1989.

- Schineller, Peter. "Shifts and Directions in Contemporary Christian Theology." *Chicago Studies* 34 (Dec. 1995): 275–90.

- Young, Frances. *Can These Dry Bones Live? An Introduction to Christian Theology.* Cleveland: Pilgrim Press, 1993.

NOTES

[1]Neil Darragh, *Doing Theology Ourselves: A Guide to Research and Action* (Auckland: Accent Publications, 1995), 28.

[2]John Macquarrie, *Principles of Christian Theology,* rev. ed. (London: SCM Press, 1986; New York: Simon & Schuster, 1985), 1.

[3]Thomas P. Rausch, in *The College Student's Introduction to Theology,* ed. Thomas P. Rausch (Collegeville, Minn.: Liturgical Press, 1993), 12.

[4]Roger Haight, *Dynamics of Theology* (New York/Mahwah, N.J.: Paulist Press, 1990), 1.

[5]Karl Rahner, *Belief Today* (New York: Sheed and Ward, 1967), 13–43.

[6]Gustavo Gutierrez, *A Theology of Liberation,* tr. C. Inda and J. Eagleson (New York: Orbis, 1973), 9.

[7]See Haight, *Dynamics of Theology,* 175–79.

[8]See, for example, *Lumen Gentium* art. 5.

[9]See Haight, Dynamies of Theology, 120–121.

[10]*Dei Verbum* art. 8.

[11]*Lumen Gentium* art.12.

[12]Howland Sanks, in *Faithful Witness: Foundations of Theology for Today's Church,* ed. T. Howland Sanks and Leo O'Donovan (New York: Crossroad, 1989), 109.

[13]Walter Kasper, *An Introduction to Christian Faith (*New York: Paulist Press, 1980), 147.

[14]A valuable survey of the different types of teaching and assent can be found in Francis A. Sullivan, *Creative Fidelity: Weighing and Interpreting Documents of the Magisterium* (New York/Mahwah, N.J.: Paulist Press, 1996), 12–27.

[15]For an overview of the theology of Thomas Aquinas, see Walter Principe's article in *Encyclopedia of Catholicism,* ed. Richard McBrien (San Francisco: Harper Collins, 1995), 83–89.

[16]Congregation for the Doctrine of the Faith, *Instruction on the Ecclesial Vocation of the Theologian* (Middlegreen: St. Paul Publications, 1990), art. 9.

[17]Karl Barth, *Revolutionary Theology in the Making: Barth-Thurneysen Correspondence, 1914–25* (London: Epworth Press, 1964), 92.

[18]Avery Dulles, *The Craft of Theology: From Symbol to System* (New York: Crossroad, 1992), 53.

[19]Rowan Williams, "Theological Integrity," *Cross Currents* 45 (1995): 322.

[20]Thomas Merton, *Seeds of Contemplation* (Wheathampstead: Anthony Clarke Books, 1972), 197–98.

Chapter Two

A HUMAN ACTIVITY

This chapter explores the shape and meaning of human existence, an important topic since it is human beings who do
theology. The chapter also examines religion as a human
phenomenon that discloses the human desire to seek meaning, purpose, and direction for our lives.

In the previous chapter, we saw that theology is grounded in the
relationship between God and humanity. The human partner in that relationship is the focus of this chapter. What it means to be human is clearly
an important issue in itself, but it is also important in the context of theology, because it is human beings who respond to the self-communication
of God by the act of faith (the subject of the next chapter). This also
means, of course, that it is human beings who do and study theology.
Accordingly, an anthropology (an understanding of what is entailed in
being human) is essential to all aspects of the project of theology. As the
contemporary American theologian Richard McBrien expresses it:

> *A theological anthropology sums up the whole of theology, for in*
> *our understanding of human existence we progressively articulate*
> *our understanding of God, of Christ, of redemption, of Church, of*
> *the moral and spiritual life. No aspect of theology is untouched by*
> *our anthropology. Therefore, no theology can begin without imme-*
> *diate attention to the question of human existence.*[1]

Theology not only deals with the relationship between God and
human beings, but it also claims to be all-inclusive; that is, as asserted

in the previous chapter, "theology excludes no human experience from its ambit." This means that theology must not only be informed by an understanding of human nature and human existence, but it must also participate in the ongoing process of deepening our awareness of what it is to be human. This is achieved in an open and critical dialogue with other disciplines such as philosophy, psychology, and sociology.

The first task that must be accomplished in this chapter is to articulate a basic understanding of what it means to be human. Having explored questions about *what* it is to be human, we will need to ask *who* a human person is; this question will involve us in the recognition of the communal quest for meaning that characterizes human existence. Our exploration of what it is to be human can begin with the simple but fundamental question: what am I?

What Am I?

Curiosity might have killed the cat, but human beings have thrived on their capacity to ask questions. To the question that heads this section, the human spirit of inquiry itself provides an initial answer: *I am a questioning being.* As parents, teachers, and students, we are all encouraged to cultivate this spirit of inquiry as a foundation for further learning. Like our children, we can always ask a further question. Humans exhibit the potential to push constantly beyond the limits of their own experience as they reflect on and scrutinize that experience. Perhaps the Roman emperor and Stoic philosopher Marcus Aurelius (121–180) provided the best formulation of the intent and direction of this process when he wrote, "Ask yourself, What is this thing in itself, by its own special constitution? What is it in substance, and in form, and in matter? What is its function in the world?"[2] Such scrutiny allows us to classify and describe what it is to be human.

The search for an answer to the question What am I? has been inseparable from the search for an answer to the question What is human nature? In this latter inquiry, we seek both to discover what it is that we share *naturally* with other human beings, irrespective of such things as ethnic and gender differentiation, and to discern the importance of the differences between humankind and other species. The ideas about human nature that emerge from such questioning are not only important to the individual who asks the question, but they also affect the shape of the society in which we live. They do so because they guide our religious aspirations and moral commitments, aspects of our lives that involve us inescapably with others.

Since issues that affect the shape of society are significant not only for us today but also for human beings in every age, it is not surprising that they have absorbed the attention of thinkers such as Socrates (470–399 B.C.E.), "the founding father" of Western philosophy, and Immanuel Kant (1724–1804), one of the principal figures of modern thought. Indeed, it was Socrates' conviction that "life without this sort of examination is not worth living."[3] For Kant, questions about matters such as human knowing and action were actually questions about the meaning of being human.[4] Such questions are essentially philosophical; we formulate our answers to them through rational inquiry, speculation, and reasoned argument.

Three Approaches to Human Nature

From the history of responses to the question, What am I? it is possible to distill three broad approaches to the *what* of human nature: the *religious,* the *philosophical,* and the *scientific.*

The *religious* approach emerged first and, as we shall see later, is present in all forms of human society. Religion viewed human nature in relation to something greater and more mysterious than itself, something that was considered to be supernatural and divine. In ancient civilizations, beliefs about fate and about divine beings and forces provided the answers to questions human beings had about their own nature and existence. Primal myths and legends portrayed gods and goddesses as responsible for the creation of the universe and as active participants in human affairs. Likewise in the monotheism of Judaism and Christianity, human beings are ultimately understood in relation to God. "God created humankind in his image" (Gen 1:27) is the basic claim of the first chapter of Genesis. Considered as "image of God," humanity is seen as being in relation to the Divine Creator and the Creator's activity. In addition, the second chapter of Genesis stresses that human beings are essentially social creatures: "It is not good that the man should be alone; I will make him a helper as his partner" (Gen 2:18). These two insights sit together happily in this religious context.

In the Greek world, however, people like Socrates began to wonder if the universe and human behavior and relationships could be explained in terms of forces other than the mysterious gods. As a consequence of their speculation, the *philosophical* approach emerged in which, without reference to religious myth and divine revelation, the universe was found to have its own inherent order and law-like structures, and in which the unique status of human nature was understood in its own terms. The Greek philosopher Protagoras of Abdera in Thrace (c.490–c.420 B.C.E.) recognized that only human beings could discover the inherent order *(logos)* of the universe when he claimed, "Humans are the measure of all things."[5]

For most philosophers up to and including Kant, two things were self-evident in this philosophical approach. First, the human being was a natural, living organism with a material body. Second, although understood as living beings, humans were different from all other beings. The human being was regarded as an animal essentially distinguished as rational.

The exercise of rational processes, evidenced in our ability to decipher mysteries and in our investigative potential, exhibited an entirely new and original phenomenon. For many philosophers, humanity shared in the possession of *Spirit (Logos* or Reason), which was considered neither to be created nor to be derived from the natural processes of the material world, and which informed the essential dignity of human nature. Thus Plato held that of all living beings, humans alone were a combination of material (body) and spiritual (soul). For Plato, as for many thinkers since, *soul* denoted everything that comprises the inner life and identity of human beings, that which is enduring and separable from merely organic existence.

By contrast, the other key figure in Greek philosophy, Aristotle (384–322 B.C.E.), rejected Plato's dualism of body and soul in favor of the constitutive unity of human nature *(anthropos)* in which material body and intellectual soul were inseparable. Aristotle took seriously the material content, the bodiliness, of human nature. As natural beings, humans are animals, possessing their own inner principle or soul *(psyche* in Greek), which organizes and directs human life and development toward its proper fulfillment (further explored in chapter 5). As rational beings, however, humans alone possess reason and self-consciousness, which belong to *nous,* the immortal part of the soul principle. For Aristotle, soul, mind, and body belong together, because the human soul actually requires bodily organs and sense experience in order to perform its rational functions in living activity.

These philosophical views of human nature were ultimately challenged by the *scientific* worldview. Relying on insights arrived at through the emergence of genetic psychology and the processes of natural and social evolution, many scientists challenged the idea that human nature was essentially different from other species. By excluding from view any possibility of essential or qualitative differences characteristic of humanity, *Homo sapiens* becomes just one animal species among many. However, as a recent product in the process of natural evolution, humans were considered quantitatively different. Humans possess a higher degree of intelligence, more organic complexity, and greater sophistication in their particular drives, energies, and capacities, evident in natural selection and adaptation. This broadly naturalistic position was adopted by the "masters of suspicion," namely Karl Marx (1809–1882), Friedrich Nietzsche (1844–1900), and Sigmund Freud (1856–1939), who called into question the distinctive character of human nature as essentially different.[6]

Those who deny that human nature is qualitatively different reduce human nature to its material processes, whether social, biological, or psychological. A scientific response to the question What am I? tends, therefore, to a one-dimensional view of human nature: we are living material beings who are in no essential way different from other beings.

These approaches indicate various perspectives from which human nature can be considered. However, as the German phenomenologist Max Scheler (1874–1928) observed, "Man is a thing so broad, variegated and diverse that all definitions turn out a little too concise. He has too many ends!"[7] Scheler's summation alerts us to the fact that "human nature" is a "weasel expression," one whose wriggles and twists reflect its subject matter.[8] No sooner do you think you have pinned a weasel word down to a single meaning, than another meaning quickly emerges, one that seems equally appropriate. This situation ought to alert us to be suspicious of any one-dimensional approach that claims to define human nature adequately.

As we have seen, the various periods in the history of thought have emphasized a variety of elements as the key to understanding human nature. Similarly, there has been a divergence of views about whether human nature is quantitatively or qualitatively different from that of other animals. In contrast to such one-dimensional thinking, the approach known as "philosophical anthropology," which was prominent from the 1920s to the 1940s, particularly in Germany, sought a philosophical elucidation of the basic qualities and conditions we share in common with other living beings as natural organisms, along with what essentially distinguishes us as human.[9] The insights of this movement will guide our discussion in the next section.

Human Nature as Multidimensional

Since it is impossible to provide a single, exhaustive definition in response to the question, What am I? an adequate consideration of human nature requires an integral understanding that embraces the fact that human nature is a complex living unity. Such an understanding needs to be inclusive; it needs to be a multidimensional approach to viewing human nature as it is. This can be achieved if we see human beings as essentially natural and social beings whose material, rational, emotional, and personal dimensions must all be respected. This integrated approach avoids the traditional oppositions such as that between mind—the more usual modern, nonreligious formulation of what was traditionally referred to as soul—and body, through the recognition of the simultaneous presence of various dimensions that together constitute the human being.

Universal agreement exists concerning our status as natural, social beings. We are embodied, and thus we share common and discernible elements with all forms of organic and inorganic life throughout the universe, such as cellular, molecular, and genetic structures. Furthermore, we are social animals whose existence is naturally and necessarily connected to levels of social organization, such as family and society. As observed by Aristotle, we are creatures who naturally live with others in a state (*polis* in Greek).[10]

As well as being material, humans are also rational. In fact, the employment of capacities such as reason, thought, and the ability to form beliefs and to have intentions and purposes, together with the mental process of logical or exact thinking that are evident in the human ability to reflect upon, to discriminate, to identify, and to relate things, constitutes for many people the determining feature of human nature. However, we should never lose sight of the interconnections between these dimensions. We are also emotional beings, capable of desire and attraction, experiencing different levels of sensations and feelings, such as fear, sympathy, friendship, and love.

Taken together, these dimensions—the material, the rational, and the emotional—inform human consciousness and our capacity to reflect on ourselves, to intend, to decide, to act, and to relate to others; and together they introduce a further dimension of the human, traditionally understood as the personal, which will be discussed in detail shortly. We can say that these dimensions, especially the first three, provide an adequate response to the questions What am I? and What is human nature? They enable us to state that humans are natural and social beings, characterized by the possession of material, rational, emotional, and personal dimensions, which together constitute a unity.

This integrated understanding of what it means to be human has significant implications for theology. Above all, it means that theology, if it is truly to be a human activity, must respect the material, social, rational, emotional, and personal dimensions of human existence and activity. It follows, for example, that a theology that required us to abandon reason entirely could not be an authentic human undertaking. Likewise, a theology that ignored the emotional and experiential aspects of human existence, or a theology pursued in isolation from community and tradition, would be alien to the context of human existence in which the drama of creation and salvation is played out.

Who Am I?

We have discerned that among the dimensions that are constitutive of the human being, a primary one is being a person. The person is characterized by self-consciousness, rationality, and the ability to make choices. These capacities give rise to a question beyond, What am I? They make possible the archetypal personal question, Who am I? This question implies a sense of identity, a developed degree of consciousness, an involvement with oneself, and a capacity for reflection, all of which inform a sense of self and the use of pronoun *I*.

In contrasting *what* and *who* questions, the distinction between objective and subjective points of view is helpful.[11] In coming to self-understanding as human beings, the objective view responds to the question, What am I? As we have seen, this question assumes an external point of view, treating ourselves as objects of scrutiny, understood as natural and social beings, consisting of various related dimensions. The question, Who am I? implies a different point of view, however; it suggests that we approach ourselves from the perspective of being a subject of experience, that we seek a self-understanding that goes beyond all possible responses to the question, What am I? For this reason, it can be argued that a person cannot be understood as a kind of object. To think or speak of someone as a person, it is necessary to use a proper name or personal pronoun. One immediately notices the difference between asking "What is Napoleon?" and asking "Who is Napoleon?"

In dealing with the self, however, we seem to be involved with another weasel expression. Many would agree with Simon Blackburn that the self is "the elusive 'I' that shows an alarming tendency to disappear when we try to inspect it."[12] The elusive nature of the person and the self is at least in part the result, as Hans Urs von Balthasar indicates, of the fact that these concepts did not emerge from a single source, but from "two very different realms: that of common sense and that of Christian theology."[13] Before we examine a modern understanding of the person, it will be valuable to look at some of the main points in the checkered history of this concept.

The History of Person: Mask, Role, Face, and Substance

While it is commonly recognized that the word *person* comes from the Latin *persona,* which refers to sound moving through or speaking through something, the actual origin and meaning of the word are obscure. The initial derivation of this expression may come from the Etruscan *phersu,* which denoted a mask or the wearer of a mask, such as an actor, at the religious festivals in honor of P(h)ersephone. The notion of a dramatic role one assumed, which implied a personal character or personality, subsequently informed the Roman understanding of the juridical person, with legal rights and duties to perform, and differentiation from mere things or property. This notion of person persists to this day.

In ancient Greece another word, *prósopon,* emerged to influence our understanding of personhood.[14] One of the words associated with the process of manifestation, it passed easily into the notion of the face or countenance of someone, which in turn connected with the Latin understanding of role and dramatic character. Hidden within this meaning was the implication in Greek thought that only humans possessed a face. Aristotle observed that the "part below the skull is named the face *(prósopon)*, but only in man, and in no other animal."[15] More significantly, the Greeks used this word as an indirect way of speaking about the second person: in saying "person," one actually said "you." This use referred to a direct face-to-face encounter between an "I and a Thou," a concept that in the twentieth century became central to the work of the Jewish philosopher and theologian Martin Buber (1878–1965).

Finally, to this network of meanings—mask, role and duties, and face—another came to be added, a meaning that is explicitly philosophical: the person as an individual substance. The Roman philosopher and politician Boethius (480–525) offered perhaps the most famous definition: "A person is the individual substance of a rational nature" *(Persona est naturae rationalis individua substantia).*[16] Although Boethius developed his ideas in a theological context, in thinking about the person of Christ, his main concern was, in fact, philosophical. As a translator of Aristotle, Boethius was familiar with the philosopher's thought and was concerned to demonstrate that *person* cannot be predicated of a *universal* substance term (for example, humanity), but only of individual substances (for example, Mary or John). Taken out of its theological context, Boethius' formula was appealing in a philosophical environment that already tended to equate the essential character of humanity with rationality. Boethius' definition informed developments during the Middle Ages that understood the dignity of human nature as personal. In addition, Boethius' work exercised a formative influence on the thinking about *person* in the early phases of the Modern Age, which focused exclusively on rational capacity.

It is worth noting that a theological concept of person was unknown to ancient pagan philosophy. The term acquired a special significance as Christians began to reflect both on the mystery of God and on the uniqueness and value of each individual human being redeemed by Christ. As people of faith began to ask, Who is God? and Who is Christ in relation to God? Christian thought made use of the concept of *prósopon/persona.* As a technical term in the theology of the Trinity and the incarnation, this concept received further connotations with respect to the role of the persons in the Trinity, and above all in their relations to one another; and these theological insights, in turn, opened up new dimensions of human thought more generally.

A key figure in this development was the Latin theologian Tertullian (c. 155–240), who pondered the distinctions within the being of God as *trinitas*. God was subsequently understood to be one "substance," but three "persons." Considered as persons in relation to each other, Father, Son, and Spirit were distinct, though sharing equally in the dignity and uniqueness of the one Godhead. Subsequent reflection on the nature of Christ, which informs traditional Christology, employed this expression in the dogma of "the one person and two natures" proclaimed by the Council of Chalcedon in 451. We will consider this development in more detail in chapter 5.

The Modern Usage of Mere Person

Not surprisingly, the use of *person* in modern thought (that is, since the seventeenth century) reflects the two major features of the modern period: first, a movement away from an integral, organic, and hierarchically structured religious worldview, in which human nature has a specific place in relation to God and other beings, and toward a worldview that posits the independence and self-sufficiency of human nature in itself; and second, the belief that human reason is the source of all explanation. In this context, priority was given to the mind and the cognitive thought processes that inform the subjective self as a center of consciousness. This idea is best represented by the famous axiom *cogito ergo sum* (I think, therefore I am), which René Descartes (1596–1650) made the foundational certainty of his philosophy.

In its modern sense, awareness of oneself as a person involves a recognition of one's identity and inherent value as a thoughtful and moral being. This is expressed in the distinction that John Locke (1632–1776) drew between *man* and *person*. Locke defined the former as simply a living organism characterized by a certain kind of biological organization; in other words, as one kind of animal among others. However, animals were not, as such, persons. A person, for Locke,

> *is a thinking, intelligent being, that has reason and reflection, and can consider itself as itself, the same thinking thing, in different times and places; which it does only by that consciousness which is inseparable from thinking and essential to it....[A]s far as this*

consciousness can be extended backwards to any past action or
thought, so far reaches the identity of that person.[17]

Although Locke's definition has had an enormous influence on contemporary social thought, it does not exhaust all possible questions about
the person. It does not tell us, for example, whether there is more to being
a person than being a thinking thing. The stress on the mind and reason
does not provide any information about such issues as the origin, the
meaning, and the purpose of personal existence. Nor does Locke's influential account do justice to the relational character of personal existence.

In reaction to the tendency to define the person exclusively as a
thinking thing, some philosophers have attempted to provide a broad definition: "the 'self' is the unity…that endures throughout change and is
aware of its unity, its endurance, and the change."[18] Yet even this broad
definition fails to emphasize that a person is essentially relational or, as
Buber has argued, "other" directed. Truly personal relationships are
between an "I" and a "Thou," so the question Who am I? can only be
addressed to another person—including, at times, oneself as a reflectively
other—for it can only be answered in terms of those other persons with
whom I am in relationship, and in terms of how my relationships with others are to be characterized and evaluated. Thus John Casey writes:

> *We can characterize as "persons" those beings who can make*
> *claims, who can incur and acknowledge obligations, can be*
> *wronged, can be the objects of and can reciprocate love, respect,*
> *hatred, and contempt.*[19]

The endeavor to reach an understanding of the person that goes
beyond an exclusive emphasis on rationality has major implications for
theology. If the person is simply an isolated, self-sufficient, thinking
thing, then the person can be understood without any reference to God,
to faith, to other people, or to any tradition of inquiry that predates and
goes beyond the questions an individual person might ask of him- or
herself. In other words, if the person is simply a thinking thing, theology ceases to have any meaning, because all of the features the previous chapter identified as fundamental to theology—the God who
reveals, the experience of faith, the community of faith, and a normative tradition—cannot be said to be central to an understanding of the
human person. If faith is peripheral to the person, then theology too is
utterly irrelevant, if not pointless. The task for the remainder of this

chapter, therefore, is to see whether it is possible to construct an understanding of the person that will justify the conviction of this book that theology is not peripheral to the human project.

Symbols as the Revelation of the Person

The eighteenth-century intellectual ferment known as the Enlightenment *(Aufklärung)* celebrated the potential of human reason freed from the shackles of religious dogma and tradition. Kant expressed the abiding spirit of this modern worldview when he declared: *"Dare to be wise! (Sapere aude!):* Have courage to use your own reasoning."[20] This audacious spirit of rational inquiry, which represented the triumph of Locke's vision of the person as a "thinking thing," transformed the existing world of thought and culture. It promoted self-reliance on the part of the individual human being and the exercise of personal freedom and responsibility in matters of morality and ultimate belief.

In our contemporary postmodern culture, however, we are more skeptical about the unrestrained powers of human reason. This skepticism is largely the product of the violence and environmental horrors of the twentieth century, experiences that have reinforced for us the conviction that authentic human existence is possible only when we embrace our interdependence and cease to insist on the merits of unrestrained individualism. In addition, psychology's emphasis on the role of the unconscious has alerted us to the fact that reason is not the sole determinant of human existence and action. Consequently, there is today a willingness to seek other emphases to guide our understanding of personal existence, emphases that are more congenial to the concerns of theology. What might these emphases be?

As was indicated at the beginning of the chapter, one of the primary features of human existence is our capacity to ask questions. This questioning reflects the fact that we are concerned about our lives and want to know what will help us to live well. We want to know what can account for our existence: If I did not bring my world and myself into being, then where did they come from? What can provide a worthwhile guide for how we are to act and an adequate explanation of the purpose or direction of our lives? In other words, we constantly seek meaning in our lives, a meaning that is not provided comprehensively by the mere reality of physical existence or even by our capacity for thinking.

Humans are able to make and remake their worlds according to their own freely chosen designs, and to embody in their works the meaning they wish to give to their world and themselves. This is evidenced clearly in the development of technology and the manufacture of tools and industrial implements that we use to increase our productive capacity. Furthermore, this resourcefulness is especially manifest in the productions of language, morality, art, and culture, which involve the creation of objects that not only have an instrumental or technical function but evoke meaning. In other words, all of these productions are symbols that take us beyond the limits of the given.

Language in particular is recognized as the key to the uniqueness of human beings and their cultural and artistic achievements. Language transcends even the most sophisticated signaling systems of the higher animals. Speech requires the exercise of intelligence combined with the intent to communicate with others; as a human phenomenon, speech is essentially social. The primary forms of speech are those of personal address, in the first and second persons: I, we, and you. We never communicate mere facts, but always facts in their significance for ourselves and those we address. Moreover, as Ludwig Wittgenstein (1889–1951), the twentieth century's foremost philosopher of language, has argued, there can be no private language for one's own private experiences, no language that is in principle intelligible only to its inventor. Essentially understood as a means of communication with others, language presupposes words, expressions, and gestures with standardized and accepted meanings. It presupposes content—what is said—but as literature, and above all poetry, remind us, language is evocative of meaning and significance that cannot be reduced to the communication of mere information.

The creation and use of symbols illustrates the importance of the notion of *intentionality* to our understanding of the human person. As a philosophical concept, intentionality is "modern in coinage but medieval in inspiration."[21] Indeed, the classic definition of intentionality comes, not surprisingly perhaps, from Thomas Aquinas: "Intention, as the name itself indicates, means to tend toward something."[22] Personal action is intentional insofar as it tends toward an object beyond itself, toward the realization of a goal, toward the attainment of a good, and above all, toward another person.

In the modern era, intentionality was creatively reappropriated by the German philosopher Franz Brentano (1838–1917). One of the inspirational figures in the philosophical movement called "phenomenology," Brentano sought to designate the distinctive feature of mental, as distinct from physical, phenomena and concluded that mental phenomena were always directed toward an object. Consciousness, therefore, is "consciousness of an object." One cannot simply be conscious; one must be conscious of something or someone. Consciousness thus presupposes both a subject and an object within a unified human experience. Every act of consciousness has a reference to something that is not itself or that is not its own activity. This fact is indicative of our capacity for openness to reality in all its forms, and above all, for openness to the reality of other persons—indeed, openness to the absolute Other considered as the sacred.

The human person is reflected in what she or he does. Furthermore, by an exercise of self-determination, intelligence, and freedom, individual human beings and communities interactively shape their personal identities. The fact that human activity engages the human person at so many levels means that action contributes far more to the project of self-revelation than does rationality considered in isolation from any other expression of what it is to be human. Thus, Karol Wojtyla (later Pope John Paul II) argues that it is in the free moral act *(actus humanus),* not simply in self-consciousness, that we reveal ourselves most specifically.[23] Wojtyla characterizes the human being, not as the rational animal, but as the "acting person."

Human persons are capable of moving beyond the constraints of what is given in their ordinary experience. We are not bound by the limits of what we are experiencing at this particular time and in this particular place. This capacity to transcend what is immediate to us, the capacity to ask "Is there more?" reveals itself in everything, from our ability to be humorous and ironic, to our ability to ask questions about what is other than us, and indeed, about what transcends us entirely: the Other.

Insofar as we are open to the world, continuing to reflect on, and question, our experience, we are searchers for the "more and the beyond," searchers for what will ultimately fulfill us, for what is always more. This search for the more, which is constitutive of the human person, is a religious quest. It not only proceeds from our desire for fulfillment, but it arises also from our desire for relief in our suffering, our desire for a power that will overcome injustice, provide guidance for the formation of morality, and ultimately offer us hope beyond our death. All of these aspects are religious. The prevalence of these religious phenomena means that our exploration of the human person cannot be regarded as complete until we grapple with the concept of religion, the final task of this chapter.

The Nature of Religion

Insofar as "theology is reflection on religion, usually undertaken by those already committed to a religious system," any consideration of theology necessarily involves an initial discussion of the idea of religion.[24] While theology has been left largely to the professionals or theologians, most people have some idea of religion. In response to the question What is religion? we are likely either to think of belief in God, supernatural spirits, and an afterlife or to name one of the great world religions, such as Hinduism or Islam.

About one hundred years ago, scholars became preoccupied with researching the origins of religion. They posed questions such as How did individuals come to believe in gods? and Has any tribe or society existed that had no form of religion? Moreover, the same spirit of inquiry that led to the emergence of anthropology as the study of human nature also facilitated the scientific study of religion.[25] This connection between the study of human nature and religion is well formulated in *Nostra Aetate,* Vatican II's Declaration on the Relation of the Church to Non-Christian Religions:

> *People look to different religions for an answer to the unsolved riddles of human existence. The problems that weigh heavily on people's hearts are the same today as in past ages. What is humanity? What is the meaning and purpose of life? What is upright behavior, and what is sinful?...And finally, what is the ultimate mystery, beyond human explanation, which embraces our entire existence, from which we take our origin and towards which we tend? (NA 1)*

The fact that religion can be said to be inextricably linked with "the human" ought to alert us to the fact that religion will not be susceptible to a simple definition. Thus, while some scholars think "religion is the human response to whatever the answer to the mystery of life is for a particular person,"[26] others caution us about claiming that we have an adequate definition of religion:

> *Definitions of religion, in a sense, remind one of the fable of the blind men attempting to define an elephant. One touches its trunk and describes it as a snake; another touches its ear and describes it as a winnowing-fan; another touches its leg and describes it as a tree; another its tail and describes it as a broom.*[27]

As with human nature, there is little agreement in determining the exact nature of religion. *Religion* is, therefore, another weasel word. Trying to define religion is like trying to define love: just about everyone knows what the word *love* means, but ask a group of people to define it, and the definitions form a quilt of multicolored, differently shaped patches, rather than a unified picture.

Although religion remains a complex human phenomenon, we recognize its universality as an enduring feature of human civilization; for notwithstanding the secularism of much contemporary culture, we have yet to discover a society that does not give meaning to human life in terms of some notion of the sacred in contrast to the profane or ordinary. The recognition of sacred times and places, sacred people, and sacred actions depends on an attitude of receptivity toward that which lies beyond human construction, control, or manipulation. The sacred or holy—expressed in symbols, myths, and ritual action—marks out boundaries and limits, thereby evoking that which lies beyond those boundaries and limits: the infinite, the all-powerful, the transcendent, a Will greater than the human will. Our "repertoire of symbols"[28]—our myths, rituals, and ways of designating the sacred—all seek in some way to evoke and name that which lies beyond ordinary experience. Hence they seek to draw the human being into a particular relationship and engagement with the sacred, with what transcends the everyday, however this transcendent reality is understood or imagined.

Accordingly, some scholars have sought to delineate religious phenomena by reflection on the etymology of the Latin noun *religio,* which designates "the religious act" or "the religious scruple, reverence, awe" directed toward, or bound to, something considered as completely other or supernatural. Three related Latin verbs offer further insight into religion: *relegere* means "to constantly turn to" or "to conscientiously observe," which implies, from the perspective of the participant, the awareness of an object of concern that deserves one's attention; *religari* means "to be bound (back)" to one's origin and goal; and *re-eligare* suggests "to choose again" to live religiously by one's origin and goal.[29] The Belgian psychoanalyst Antoine Vergote suggests that these etymological meanings proposed for the term *religion* meet and fulfill each other through the human response to the sacred in the act of faith expressed within a community.[30]

In short, anthropological and sociological considerations suggest that the religious impulse in human beings should be understood as arising from the desire to find ultimate meaning and purpose in life. Religion expresses the awareness that we are not self-sufficient, that we ourselves are not a sufficient explanation for the existence and shape of the universe. Religion also links us to others who are seeking meaning, and thus it confirms the social dimension of our existence.

For Christians, the receptivity to the sacred expressed in the religious impulse finds its completion in an explicit act of faith in response to God. As we will see in the next chapter, theology is grounded in this faith response, which is essentially the surrender of ourselves to what provides the ultimate fulfilment for human existence. Theology seeks to articulate the reasons for that response so that believers themselves may appropriate it more thoughtfully and willingly and so that nonbelievers may be given some insight into the nature of faith. At the heart of Christian faith is the conviction that God is revealed definitively in Jesus Christ, and hence that faith in Jesus Christ is a response to God's self-revelation or self-communication. The examination of this fundamental claim, then, is the agenda for the next chapter.

QUESTIONS FOR REFLECTION

1. How are the various dimensions of human nature related?

2. What challenges do contemporary developments in the human and physical sciences raise for our understanding of *person?*

3. What are some experiences that have made you aware of your desire for what is "more"?

4. What elements would you include in a definition of *religion?*

SUGGESTIONS FOR FURTHER READING

- Gelpi, Donald L. *The Turn to Experience in Contemporary Theology.* New York: Paulist Press, 1994.

- Hill, Brennan R., Paul Knitter, and William Madges. *Faith, Religion, and Theology: A Contemporary Introduction.* Mystic, Conn.: Twenty-Third Publications, 1995.

- Lopston, Peter. *Theories of Human Nature.* Petersborough, Ontario: Broadview Press, 1995.

- Murdoch, Iris. *The Sovereignty of Good.* London: Routledge, 1996.

NOTES

[1]Richard McBrien, *Catholicism,* rev. ed. (North Blackburn, Victoria: Collins Dove, 1994; San Francisco: Harper San Francisco, 1994), 75.

[2]Marcus Aurelius, *Meditations* VIII, 11, tr. Maxwell Staniforth (London: Penguin, 1964), 123.

[3]Plato, "Apology" 38A, in *The Last Days of Socrates,* tr. Hugh Tredennick and Harold Tarrant (London: Penguin Books, 1993; New York: Viking Penguin, 1993), 63.

[4]Immanuel Kant, "Logik" A26, in Herbert Schnädelbach, *Philosophy in Germany, 1831–1933* (Cambridge, U.K.: Cambridge University Press, 1984), 220.

[5]Harry A. Ide, "The Sophists," in *The Cambridge Dictionary of Philosophy,* ed. Robert Audi (Cambridge, U.K.: Cambridge University Press, 1995), 752.

[6]Paul Ricoeur, *Freud & Philosophy: An Essay on Interpretation,* tr. Denis Savage (New Haven, Conn.: Yale University Press, 1970), 32.

[7]Max Scheler, "On the Idea of Man," *Journal of the British Society for Phenomenology* 9 (October 1978): 185.

[8]This meaning of "weasel expression" comes from Donald L. Gelpi, *The Turn to Experience in Contemporary Theology* (New York: Paulist Press, 1994), 2.

[9]Howard Kainz, *The Philosophy of Man* (Tuskaloosa, Ala.: University of Alabama Press, 1981), 3–6.

[10]Aristotle, *The Nicomachean Ethics* I,7, tr. J. A. K. Thompson (London: Penguin Books, 1953), 37.

[11]Thomas Nagel, *Mortal Questions* (Cambridge, U.K.: Cambridge University Press, 1979), 196f.

[12]Simon Blackburn, *The Oxford Dictionary of Philosophy* (Oxford: Oxford University Press, 1994), 344.

[13]Hans Urs von Balthasar, "On the Concept of Person," *Communio* 13 (Spring 1986): 18.

[14]Kenneth L. Schmitz, "The Geography of the Human Person," *Communio* 13 (Spring 1986): 29–30.

[15]Aristotle, "Historia animalium" 491 b9–11, in Schmitz, "Geography," 30.

[16]Boethius, "Liber de persona et duabus naturis contra Eutychen et Nestorium" 111, in *Patrologiae cursus completus,* ed. J.-P Migne (Paris: Vraet de Surgy, 1847), 64:1343.

[17]John Locke, *An Essay Concerning Human Understanding*, ed. A. D. Woozley (Glasgow: Collins/Fount Paperbacks, 1977), 211–12.

[18]Peter A. Angeles, *Dictionary of Philosophy* (New York: Barnes & Noble Books, 1981), 251.

[19]John Casey, *Pagan Virtue: An Essay in Ethics* (Oxford: Clarendon Press, 1990), 2.

[20]Immanuel Kant, "An Answer to the Question: 'What Is Enlightenment?'" in *Kant's Political Writings,* tr. H. B. Nisbet (Cambridge, U.K.: Cambridge University Press, 1971), 54.

[21]H. B. Veatch, "Intentionality," in *New Catholic Encyclopedia,* vol 7 (New York: McGraw-Hill, 1967), 564.

[22]*Summa Theologiae* 1a 2ae, 12.1.

[23]Karol Wojtyla, *The Acting Person*, written in collaboration with Anna-Teresa Tymieniecka, tr. Andrzej Ptooki (Dordrecht: D. Reidel Publishing Co,

1979). See also his article, "The Intentional Act and the Human Act That Is Act and Experience," *Analecta Husserliana* 10 (1976): 269–80.

[24]John F. Haught, *What Is Religion? An Introduction* (New York: Paulist Press, 1990), 9.

[25]See Clinton Bennett, *In Search of the Sacred: Anthropology and the Study of Religion* (London: Cassell, 1996).

[26]Ronald J. Wilkins, *Religions of the World* (Dubuque: Wm. C. Brown Company, 1984), 9.

[27]Eric J. Sharpe, *Understanding Religion* (London: Duckworth, 1983), 46.

[28]Ninian Smart, *Dimensions of the Sacred* (London: HarperCollins, 1996; Berkeley, Calif.: University of California Press, 1996), 1.

[29]Norbert Schiffers, "Religion, Concept of; Religion in General," in *Encyclopedia of Theology: A Concise Sacramentum Mundi*, ed. Karl Rahner (London: Burns & Oates, 1975; New York: Crossroad, 1975), 1359.

[30]Antoine Vergote, *Guilt and Desire: Religious Attitudes and Their Pathological Derivations*, tr. M. H. Wood (New Haven, Conn.: Yale University Press, 1988), 129.

Chapter Three

GROUNDED IN FAITH

> This chapter focuses on the fact that theology is done within a faith tradition. We will explore the relationship between faith and revelation and also the way God's self-revelation in Jesus and the Spirit forms a community of faith. We will see that faith, if it is not to become a dead letter, must be experienced as a word about the situation of the believer, and must offer the promise of an absolute future.

In chapter 1, we considered various definitions of theology. Those definitions not only gave us some idea of the range of theological inquiry and activity but also alerted us to the fact that theology is grounded in faith, for each of the definitions related to faith in one way or another. The first two definitions referred to the content and the experience of faith, aspects that theology has named the *fides quae* (the faith that is believed) and the *fides qua* (the faith by which we believe) respectively. The former refers to faith in an objective sense; the latter refers to faith in a subjective sense. Another way this distinction has been expressed is by referring to the former as "beliefs" and the latter as "faith."[1] We will not be too concerned about the semantics, but we do want to look at the relationship between these two aspects of faith. Put simply, both aspects are about naming our experience of God. In so doing, we are looking for appropriate language to speak the truth about God. This is what we mean by doing theology, the focus of this chapter.

We cannot speak of faith, however, without also considering revelation. In other words, we are concerned about God's action in the dynamic that is faith. How does God choose to reveal Godself? How is the truth about God communicated to the world? To attempt to answer these questions is to engage in a theological activity; it is about finding the right words to express the mode of God's self-revelation or self-communication. Both of these expressions—self-revelation and self-communication—are used by theologians to describe the process by which God makes Godself known to human beings; we will use them interchangeably in the pages that follow.

The definitions we considered in chapter 1 also showed us that the task of theology is the task of a community. The community may seek out the truth of all reality by means of its religious symbols; it also engages in reflection on its day-to-day situation and experience and on its pastoral activity. Here again, theology is grounded in faith. The life and experience of the community give rise to a particular way of putting the experience of God into words. In this sense, it is possible to speak of the "faith of the church." This expression is not meant to convey the idea that the faith is the possession of some group of experts or authority figures who are removed from our daily experience. On the contrary, the faith of the Church is the faith of the people. Finding the right language to express that faith is as challenging for the present generation as it was for previous generations. As we will see later in this chapter, telling the story of the faith is important for the life of the community.

Thus, in this chapter we will not only examine some of the building blocks that allow us to do theology, but we will also engage in the task of doing theology as we explore these aspects of the Christian experience and story.

The Experience of Faith

All believing Christians would acknowledge that they have some experience of God. For some it may come through prayer or the celebration of the liturgy. These people would tell us about the experience of being transported beyond themselves to something higher, or of being confident that God was present to them in a sacramental action, or simply that their prayers were answered and they knew that God loved them and cared for them.

Some people experience God in what would be considered secular settings. These people can recount how their most intense experiences of the presence of God occurred as they watched the sun setting

over the ocean, or when they stood on an alpine height towering above
the clouds and knew then the majesty of the Creator God. Some people,
reminiscent of Elijah in the Old Testament (cf. 1 Kgs 19:11–13), would
indicate that they experienced God in the deepest moments of peaceful-
ness or stillness. Their experience was one of well-being and whole-
ness, a time when life seemed to be all together and just right.

Some people come to know God through the experience of reading poetry or looking at a beautiful piece of art. For these people, the
experience is at once both intellectual and affective. Often the experience can be one of pain as the reader or observer enters into the grief or
agony conveyed by the artist. Of course, many people will tell us that
some of their most difficult and painful moments of life were the most
purifying for them and gave them a new vision. We are probably all
familiar with the experience of someone who has watched a loved one
suffer and die over a long period of time. They may have cursed God as
they saw what was happening, they may have questioned the reality of
God if such suffering could occur, but they also may have come to a
resolution of their pain and anger and deepened their faith in God.

This raises a difficulty about speaking of religious experience or of
experiences of God or even of faith. If some people tell us that they deepened their faith in God as a result of pain or suffering, there are many
more people who would tell us that they stopped believing in God as a
result of such experiences or of the atrocities that beset our world. Similarly, watching a beautiful sunset may lead some people to experience
God, but for more people it is simply a good experience that has nothing
to do with God. God is not necessary to explain it, nor is faith in God
essential to the experience. Likewise those who read poetry or visit art
galleries probably do not do these things with the hope of discovering
God. This suggests to us that faith is not compelled merely by human
experience; something beyond ourselves is needed before we can name
the experience a religious experience. The defining characteristic of a
religious experience is that, within the human experience, God is to be
found. In other words, religious faith is a response to God's desire to be
known by human beings and to be known in human experience.

Thus, if God's initiative is always prior to any human response, it
follows that faith in God, while it inescapably involves our personal
decision and commitment, is not primarily a human endeavor; it is a
response to God's invitation. Christians would certainly claim that the

God in whom they believe is a God who meets the fundamental human desire that was discussed in the previous chapter, namely, the desire for something greater than ourselves to be the source of meaning for our lives, to provide hope and comfort in the midst of suffering or in the face of death; but they would reject any suggestion that they have constructed God to meet these desires.

Christians would argue that their faith in God, far from being wish fulfillment, is a response to God's own invitation in Jesus Christ to find in God their source of meaning, security, hope, and vision. Indeed, Christians believe that the very desire for something more, which might seem to be merely a human desire, manifests the truth that human beings can be fulfilled only in union with God. Clearly, one of the tasks of this chapter is to show why such claims, far from being absurd or incomprehensible, are worthy of respect.

There are many people who want to restrict the initiative of God and the experience of faith to an overtly religious setting. They would claim that faith is experienced and lived out as a knowledge of God, and that this is taught primarily by means of the doctrines of the church and its liturgy. This position raises a fundamental question about our understanding of faith and of the revelation of God, a question theologian Bernard Cooke has addressed in his book *The Distancing of God.*[2] Cooke argues that the world and human experience should be considered as a primary locus for the revelation of God, and that a restriction of revelation or religious experience to sacred times or places or texts amounts to a "distancing" of God. Even though such a distancing developed within the first couple of centuries of Christianity, the earliest Christian experience was of a God who was present in daily living. The life of St. Augustine is a good example of the dynamic interaction between human experience and the initiative of God.

The Religious Experience of St. Augustine

When we turn to Augustine's *Confessions,* his spiritual autobiography, we notice that his experience reaches an intensity in Book 8, in which he recounts his misery and pain as he tries to deal with his own struggle to believe. The language is powerful: all his misery is dredged out of the secret recesses of his soul and "heaped in full view" of his heart; this leads to a "mighty storm" within and "a mighty downpour of tears." He feels intense isolation in this experience; although he is surrounded by long-standing friends and confidants, he is alone as he lives through the ordeal he is facing.

Augustine writes of throwing himself on the ground under a tree and just allowing the tears to burst forth. Unable to control himself and his emotions, he cries out, asking how long this can go on. Will it finish later today or tomorrow or when? At this point of desperation, he hears the voices of children playing in a neighboring yard. The words of their rhyming game seem to say to him, "Take and read." This becomes a turning point in his experience because he hears these words as words of hope. He picks up his Bible and reads whatever is open before him. Just a few sentences are enough to calm him, a peaceful light pours into his heart, and "all the dark shadows of doubt fle[e] away." He immediately runs to one of his friends to tell what has happened, and the friend helps him to appreciate the significance of his conviction that God has spoken to him. He concludes the description of this experience in Book 10 of the *Confessions* with one of the most celebrated passages in Christian literature:

> *Late have I loved you, beauty so old and so new: late have I loved you. And see, you were within me and I was in the external world and sought you there, and in my unlovely state I plunged into those lovely created things which you made. You were with me, and I was not with you. The lovely things kept me far from you, though if they did not have existence in you, they had no existence at all. You called and cried out loud and shattered my deafness. You were radiant and resplendent, you put to flight my blindness. You were fragrant, and I drew in my breath and now pant after you. I tasted you, and I feel but hunger and thirst for you. You touched me, and I am set on fire to attain the peace which is yours.*[3]

Here we see the complexity of Christian faith and get a glimpse of one of the most difficult questions with which theologians have grappled for almost the whole of Christian history, namely, the relationship between God's grace and human freedom in coming to faith. Clearly, Augustine acknowledges that all his own efforts to encounter God were worthless without an initiative on God's part to open his eyes and his ears. All the experiences of his life had been useless and had in fact kept God at a distance until that time when there was a meeting of God's desires for him and his own free will. It was as though there was a barrier to be broken: Augustine was on one side trying to break through to God, and God was on the other side trying to break through to Augustine. Ironically, their efforts had seemed to be at cross-purposes. Augustine finally encountered God when he became free enough and open enough to see and hear God in his own heart without setting the terms for belief. This was the great insight he placed on the opening page of the *Confessions:* "You have made us for yourself and our hearts are restless until they rest in you." Faith is about the human heart in its restlessness; it is about the gradual resolution of that restlessness, which is encounter with God.

Some of these ideas are reflected on more soberly by Augustine in a passage from his commentary on John's Gospel in a section dealing with the words "No one can come to me unless drawn by the Father" (Jn 6:44). This is about God's desires and the desires of the human heart. For Augustine, persons should be attuned to the desires of their hearts; they should recognize their hungers and thirsts. He identifies a fundamental fact of human life, a fact that expresses the human capacity for transcendence that we discussed in the previous chapter: we delight in truth, in happiness, in holiness, and in eternal life. This is the level where faith is operating, even if at times we are unable to name it explicitly as faith. In the experiences of life, declares Augustine, God is ultimately encountered:

> Give me one who loves, and he feels what I am saying. Give me one who desires, give me one who hungers, give me one travelling and thirsting in this solitude and sighing for the fountain of an eternal homeland, give me such a one, and he knows what I am saying. But if I speak to someone coldly unresponsive, he knows not what I speak.[4]

For Augustine the experience of faith is linked to the passion for living.

A Theology of Faith

Augustine's idea of the restlessness of the human heart has a prominent place in contemporary theologies of faith. It is considered as part of the fundamental structure of the human person, and it points to the spiritual dimension of human existence. We have already considered this idea in the previous chapter; here we will explore it in terms of faith. We are capable of reaching out beyond ourselves in situations such as loving another, being overcome with joy or sadness, making a decision that sets our life on a particular course, or choosing to do good. Similarly, we may feel vulnerable in the face of the world around us; we may ask the most fundamental questions about the meaning of life, about the future, and about existence beyond death. These experiences and these questions push us toward an ultimate reality beyond ourselves; we either conclude that life is meaningless, or we surrender in fundamental trust. This surrender is an act of self-transcendence; it expresses what it is to be fully human. It is part of the experience of all people and arises out of concrete situations that are determined by such things as history, culture, and circumstances.

At this stage in our discussion, we need to consider the point to which the person is reaching out. It has to be a point that is absolutely beyond the self. Because it is a striving for the infinite or "the more," as was described in the previous chapter, this reaching out can be satisfied only by the transcendent absolute. This is where that fundamental trust is located. Theology helps us name this transcendent absolute as God. The process of coming to Christian faith thus involves a movement from implicit faith, where we live out of that fundamental trust, to an explicit faith, where we can name God. There is a real sense in which this move requires a "leap of faith"; it will never end with rational knowledge, such as the knowledge that the earth is round. Arrival at the point of explicit faith, however, should not entail an irrational act. We will explore this point a little later within the context of revelation.

Here we can refer to God as the object of our faith, and in so doing we bring God into the dynamic of our coming to explicit faith. Theology discusses this under the heading of *grace*. That our reaching beyond ourselves puts us in touch with the transcendent absolute is something that is necessarily beyond our own powers; it has to be something that is given to us. This freely given gift is called grace. Theology has other ways of discussing this. For example, it speaks of God's free gift of the Holy Spirit. In the Pauline literature of the New Testament, we discover a theology of the "spiritual person." This is the person who has received the Spirit of God, which bears witness with our spirit; and by this Spirit we have been made "children" of God (Rom 8). From this piece of theological reflection we are able to draw the conclusion (which is not at odds with what we have said above about human self-transcendence) that the experience of faith is ultimately an experience of being drawn into the life of God. Or, to take up an ancient idea, the experience of faith is the experience of being "divinized." This is quite clearly the result of an action on the part of God; it is grace. Another way theology speaks of faith is as a response to *revelation,* the initiative on God's part to communicate and open up for the person the possibility of divine encounter.

Revelation as the Self-Disclosure of God

The biblical narrative of Abraham is one of the most venerable accounts of God's self-revelation and of the human response to it. It presents us with a very dynamic relationship existing between God and Abraham. We shall begin by considering the Abraham narrative itself. Later we shall consider it as a narrative kept alive by a people as a way of remembering their history—a history that becomes not only salvation history but also the means for the continuing self-revelation of God.

In the Abraham narrative, we are struck immediately by the fact that God communicates to Abraham and promises him a future. We hear of words that suggest speech on God's part: the Lord "said" to Abraham, or the word of the Lord "came" to Abraham. We should avoid the temptation, however, of seeing this in purely extrinsic terms, as though God's revelation is simply something that impinges on Abraham from outside or necessarily comes like a bolt of lightning. What these phrases suggest (and what biblical scholarship is able to demonstrate) is that God's self-revelation takes place in history. Abraham's personal history was thus the vehicle for the encounter with God. References to such things as his experience of being childless, his gazing at the stars, his nomadic existence, and his offering ritual sacrifice all give us the context in which God's self-revelation took place. Through them, Abraham saw the mighty works of God. In other words, they point to the *what* of revelation.

What God revealed was a promise, a promise that Abraham would become a great nation, that he would have many descendants, that there would be a future for him and his descendants, and that they would live with security. What God revealed, of course, was God. This narrative represents the beginning of the attempt by a people to name God. The naming of God is only possible because of the self-revelation of God, which, as the narrative suggests, has taken place for Abraham in his life and his history. Abraham's experience was of the "transcendent absolute" beyond himself, a mystery that was expressed in the promise of God.

Equally as important as God's word to Abraham was Abraham's response. This has come down to us as the obedience of faith and has led to references to Abraham as our "father in faith" (cf. Rom 4:16). This faith is a response of trust and of hope. Paul puts it simply: "Abraham believed in God, and it was reckoned to him as righteousness" (Rom 4:3, cf. Gen 15:6). There is a sense here that the promise is fulfilled in its acceptance, and that other names for the promise, for God's self-revelation, are "righteousness" or "justice" or "salvation." The God revealed here is the God who offers salvation, which really is about having a future—and an ultimate future at that.

Revealed in the Memory of a People

The bibilical text that has come down to us, as we will see in the next chapter, was handed down over many generations. Hence we can speak of revelation not only as the self-revelation of God to Abraham, but also as the self-revelation of God to the people of Israel in their history. Consider the following passage in the Abraham story:

> Then the LORD said to Abram, "Know this for certain, that your off-spring shall be aliens in a land that is not theirs, and shall be slaves there, and they shall be oppressed for four hundred years; but I will bring judgment on the nation that they serve, and afterward they shall come out with great possessions. As for yourself, you shall go to your ancestors in peace; you shall be buried in a good old age. And they shall come back here in the fourth generation; for the iniquity of the Amorites is not yet complete." (Gen 15:13–16)

This passage is quite clearly the promise made to Abraham, but for the people now listening to it or reading it, it is a promise that has already been fulfilled. The story was in fact a memorial of God's mighty works. It was heard as a word that interpreted their own history as the history of God's promises being fulfilled. In that history God's self-revelation has continued, and the people have come to know God and to name God.

What we are seeing is thus an interplay between God's word and

God's works, both of which constitute God's self-revelation. Equally important, both word and works belong to the history of this people and to their memory. There is now a dynamic interplay between the past, the present, and the future. The God who has been revealed in their history and who is revealed in the present is the same God who offers a promise for the future. The response of the people toward this promise is not some irrational or mindless hope. It is based on the confidence that has been built up in the mighty works of God fulfilled in their lives and the lives of their ancestors.

God is revealed as the God who offers a future to this people. The response to this revelation is for the people to give an account of their hope. In fact, the sacred writings of these people are such an account. Hope thus builds on hope as the self-revelation of God unfolds in the memory of the people.

The promise of God and the hope of the people are sealed in the covenant. It thus gradually becomes clearer *who* God is: one who is faithful, just, and upright. The Song of Moses (Dt 32) celebrates the God of the covenant. In what is no doubt a ritual action, the name of the Lord is proclaimed, the people remember the God of their ancestors, and the history of God's self-revelation through mighty works is told:

> *He sustained [Jacob] in a desert land,*
> *in a howling wilderness waste;*
> *he shielded him, cared for him,*
> *guarded him as the apple of his eye.*
> *As an eagle stirs up its nest,*
> *and hovers over its young;*
> *as it spreads its wings, takes them up,*
> *and bears them aloft on its pinions,*
> *the LORD alone guided him;*
> *no foreign god was with him.*
> *He set him atop the heights of the land,*
> *and fed him with produce of the field;*
> *he nursed him with honey from the crags,*
> *with oil from flinty rock;*
> *curds from the herd, and milk from the flock,*
> *with fat of lambs and rams;*
> *Bashan bulls and goats,*
> *together with the choicest wheat—*
> *you drank fine wine from the blood of grapes. (Dt 32:10–14)*

Jesus: The Definitive Self-Communication of God

Throughout the long history of this people, God continued to be revealed, the promise made to their ancestors became more transparent, and the meaning of salvation became clearer. Jesus was born among this people; he is part of their history. Through his preaching and mighty works, the self-revelation of God continued and was brought to completion. Now, both the promise and its meaning as salvation are seen in the person of Jesus himself. In him the history of the people continues as the history of God's words and God's works, that is, of God's revelation.

The ministry of Jesus is characterized by gestures that reveal God as one who is faithful, just, and upright. The word of the Lord comes to those whom Jesus encounters as a word of both promise and fulfillment. Thus, a paralytic is cured, a blind man sees, the deaf hear, lepers are cleansed, and sinners are forgiven. All of these are revelatory signs that point to God as the true hope of the people. They reveal a God who is breaking into the world in a definitive manner, or—to use the words of Jesus' proclamation—they reveal the dawning of the reign of God. It is true to say that this revelation comes through the person of Jesus; he is central to it.

As we hear the Gospel accounts, we are conscious that the people were gradually becoming aware that in Jesus a new image of God was being revealed to them. Jesus speaks among them as one with authority. A good example of this is in the account of Jesus calming the storm (Mk 4:35–41). The episode ends with the question from the disciples: "Who then is this, that even the wind and the sea obey him?" Jesus' actions are seen as belonging to the realm of God, who is the creator of the wind and the sea and all of creation. Likewise, when Jesus forgives sin, he is asked by what authority he does this, because God alone can forgive sin (Mk 2:7). Here again, we see how the actions of Jesus are seen as belonging to the realm of God—this time God as Savior.

The Gospels, however, indicate that it is more than the actions of Jesus that reveal God; God is also revealed in the very person of Jesus. The message revealed to Abraham and earlier generations is now even more clearly perceived. Essentially that message is that God is with the people, that God stands in solidarity with them, and that God offers them an absolute future. This is nowhere more apparent than in the death of Jesus.

Here is the ultimate act of fidelity on the part of God. In all of the drama and tragedy of Jesus' death, we witness the most telling account of the promise of God and its fulfillment in the resurrection. That promise is thus expressed in terms of an absolute future that transcends the limitations of the mundane and offers an ultimate answer to the most basic, as well as the most dire, of all human questioning. This act of God has established the final and definitive covenant between God and humanity, a covenant that creates and sustains humanity in communion with God.

Jesus: The Definitive Human Response to God

One aspect of revelation that we need to look at in more detail emerges out of that fundamental datum of revelation, the incarnation. By and large in the above discussion, we have been focusing on the person of Jesus as the self-revelation of God. The incarnation, however, also states that Jesus is fully human. We have already considered some of the implications of this statement by claiming an absolute future for humanity based on the consequences of Jesus' own life, death, and resurrection. We must also claim that in Jesus we see the definitive human response, which we referred to earlier, when speaking of Abraham, as the "obedience of faith." In other words, we see in Jesus the ultimate experience of faith that we discussed at the beginning of this chapter.

One of the best glimpses we get of Jesus as the person of faith is in the garden scene before his death. Faced with his impending and violent death, Jesus is seen struggling with the promise of God. This becomes a real test of the fidelity of God toward him, just as much as it is a test of his obedient response of faith. Here in the garden, Jesus is called to give an account of his hope in the most practical and radical way. The language of Mark's Gospel (Mk 14:33–36) captures the tension involved as Jesus makes his response: Jesus is distressed and agitated; he is deeply grieved, even to the point of death; he throws himself on the ground and prays that things might be different; finally, he addresses God as "Abba, Father" and entrusts himself to the providence of this God.

For Jesus, what is at stake is the very core of his preaching about God and the reign of God, the very self-revelation of God. If Jesus cannot respond in faith to this revelatory moment, then he cannot be the revelation of God. If he cannot respond in faith, then there can be neither promise nor future. From the theological point of view, it thus becomes clear that faith and revelation belong together as two sides of one coin. The self-revelation of God presupposes a response of faith if it is to be truly a self-communication; faith is only possible on the basis of God's self-revelation as a God who is faithful, just, and upright.

We see this juxtaposition of faith and revelation throughout the ministry of Jesus. On the many occasions of encounter between Jesus and those who follow him, Jesus opens up horizons of possibility for them not simply through gestures of healing and saving, but also by calling them to faith. In fact, the statement that "your faith has saved you," or the challenge to have more faith, is fundamentally a call to trust God, especially when there seems no other reasonable response. This is what Paul referred to as "hoping against hope" (Rom 4:18).[5] It is also what we have seen of Jesus' own life, especially in the garden scene. The follower of Jesus, then, is one who not only takes Jesus as the model of faith but also accepts Jesus as the catalyst for faith. As such, Jesus is recognized as the definitive revelation of God and the model of the obedient response of faith.

The Faith of the Church

Thus far, we have generally been working from narratives (the stories of Abraham and Jesus) to explore both the experience and the content of faith. These narratives, as has already been suggested, belong to a people; they are their sacred memories of the promises of God and the fulfillment of those promises. Narrative is a useful way of expressing faith because it gradually opens up the mystery of God to us. We can tell and retell the stories and discover each time new depths of meaning. The early Christian community did just this as it tried to make sense of what had happened to Jesus. Thus Paul, as we saw above in the reference to Romans 4, took the story of Abraham and reread it in the light of the revelation of Jesus and the faith of the community of his followers. Narrative is a powerful means of belonging to a group, and God was known and named as the God of the group. Hence we find references to the God of the ancestors, the God of Abraham, Isaac, and Jacob, and eventually to the God of Jesus (e.g., Rom 15:6; Eph 1:17).

Among the first Christians, certain stories of Jesus became pivotal in the process of coming to faith. Some of the most well-developed of these appear in the fourth Gospel. For example, the story of Jesus and the Samaritan woman at the well (Jn 4:7–42) is a progressive unfolding of who Jesus is, and it shows how the woman gradually comes to know the person of Jesus and to discover his true identity. She begins by simply referring to him as a Jew; then she acknowledges him as a prophet; next as the Messiah. In the conversation, Jesus has gradually been revealing himself: first as someone who is thirsty, then as one who can offer her fresh, living water—water that promises her a secure future. Next, he reveals that he knows something of the woman's own story. And finally, in revealing himself as the Messiah, he uses a phrase that links him directly to the divine name: "I am" (cf. Ex 3:13–15). The next stage of the narrative tells, among other things, that many people from the woman's city came to believe in Jesus on the basis of her testimony; and eventually they put their faith into words, saying, "This is truly the Savior of the world" (Jn 4:42).

This narrative and others like it were important instruments of catechesis in the Johannine community; they helped people both to know and to experience the faith of that community. In other words, the faith resided in the community, and new people were continually being initiated into the group. This is what we mean when we speak of faith as the faith of the church. It is not surprising, then, that these narratives, which lived on in the written and oral tradition, were central in the process of new believers coming to faith and preparing for baptism. They are still used today in a similar way in the lectionary for the season of Lent as catechumens prepare for baptism.

The opening verses of the first letter of John (1 Jn 1:1–3) express these same ideas in a very different way:

> *We declare to you what was from the beginning, what we have heard, what we have seen with our eyes, what we have looked at and touched with our hands, concerning the word of life—this life was revealed, and we have seen it and testify to it, and declare to you the eternal life that was with the Father and was revealed to us—we declare to you what we have seen and heard so that you also may have fellowship with us; and truly our fellowship is with the Father and with his Son Jesus Christ.*

The point here is that the faith is found in the fellowship, the *koinonia*, among the people and with God.

The People's Instinct for the Faith

The Johannine literature explains *koinonia* in terms of the anointing of the Spirit (cf. 1 Jn 2:20, 27). The Spirit abides with the believers in the community, enabling them to recognize the truth. As we have seen in the first chapter, the church is the place where the Spirit is alive. To speak of the faith of the church is to speak about the instinct for the faith that is present in the people of God because they are a Spirit-filled people.

The fourth Gospel provides us with sufficient data to develop a theological explanation of this important idea that the faith of the church resides in the instinct of the people. In his farewell speech, Jesus promises to send the Spirit among his disciples to teach them the truth and to remind them of all that he has taught them (Jn 14:26). The Spirit is thus present as the active memory of the church. We have already referred to the importance of memory among the Hebrew people as the source of the self-revelation of God. This memory is clearly anchored in the dynamic life of the Spirit among the people. Through the Spirit, the church is able to keep alive the memory of the works and words of Jesus. Given that the covenant established between God and the people in the death of Jesus is definitive, the work of the Spirit is best understood as leading the people to a deeper involvement in the mystery of God revealed in Jesus. They are able to penetrate its meaning for living in the contemporary situation. The instinct for the faith, then, is not essentially about devising the right formulas of faith (although it does not exclude this), but about being able to comprehend the significance of Jesus' words and works in ever-changing situations.

Later in the same discourse, Jesus speaks of this in terms of truth. The Spirit will guide the believer into the truth (Jn 16:13). Truth here is more than doctrinal truth; it is the truth of the self-revelation of God. It is fundamentally the truth about the person of God and the promises made to the people. The Spirit, then, orients the people toward the future. The Spirit acts as both reminder and guarantor of that future. Under the influence of the Spirit, the people are able to work out their future. This seems to be exactly what Paul was speaking of when he referred to the "spiritual person" and to spiritual maturity.

The relationship between truth and faith is well explored by the idea of *sensus fidei* (a sense of the faith), which has always had an important place in the church's language about faith. The Second Vatican Council's Dogmatic Constitution on the Church, *Lumen Gentium,* declares that "the whole body of the faithful who have received an anointing which comes from the holy one cannot be mistaken in belief" (LG 12). It refers to this quality as a "supernatural sense of the faith," which is "aroused and sustained by the Spirit of truth."

The German theologian Herbert Vorgrimler is one of many theologians to explore how this instinct for the faith can become a genuine consensus among the faithful. He reaches the conclusion that such a consensus will be best realized in both narrative form and praxis:

> *It is easier to say what consensus is if, instead of thinking of the faith's articulation in propositions ("theories" in this sense), we consider the concrete performance of faith in terms of human life.*[6]

Such a position takes full account of the breadth of meaning we have given to the idea of faith throughout this chapter. It also appreciates that the truth of the faith transcends words. This was an understanding that was crystal clear to the earliest generations of believers. Although there was a profession of faith at the time of baptism, these words were only possible because the person was already beginning to live "in the truth." For this reason, the more formal catechesis in the truths of the faith took place after baptism.

The sort of consensus we are speaking of is a sign of the *koinonia* referred to above in the first letter of John. In this sense, it is valid to claim that the unity in faith of the church is a gift of the Holy Spirit. Each generation, however, has to make that unity an existential reality among its own people and in its own place.

Symbolic Expression

Although narrative and praxis are important ways in which the faith of the people is known, experienced, and expressed, there are other important ways of expressing something that is ultimately very difficult to express. The allusion earlier to baptism points us to another significant way of expressing the faith of the church: symbols. The narrative of the Samaritan woman at the well developed around the themes of water and baptism. The fundamental image here is of a spring of water, which not only is refreshing and able to quench thirst but gives and sustains life. The telling of the story was not so much concerned with conveying the truth about God in a thematic and systematic way as it was about drawing people into the experience of encounter with the God of Jesus. The truth was not simply known in propositional form, but as something that transcended propositions, something to which believers were continually reaching out. This power of symbol reminds us of what has been alluded to in the first two chapters: that symbols are as necessary to the life of faith as they are to life in general.

The experience of the first believers was rich in symbol. Indeed, the meaning of their faith was expressed most significantly and poignantly in two symbolic rituals: baptism and eucharist. Each of these rituals in its own way affirmed that the fullness of God's revelation was to be found in the mystery of the Christ event. Both presumed the participation of the people in this event. The power of symbol was that it could connect the events of the past, which had formed the faith of their ancestors, and the promise of a future, with the life of people in the present. Faith, expressed symbolically, communicated truth—but truth that was as much about a way of life as it was about a formula of words.

Nevertheless, words were important for expressing the faith of the people. Words always accompanied symbolic actions as a word of interpretation and a word of faith. Those being baptized were asked questions about their faith as a way of affirming that the faith they professed was the faith of the church. These were not elaborate formulations, but simple statements of the core of the mystery of faith. In the case of those being baptized, it amounted to a series of questions inquiring about belief in God as Father, Son, and Spirit. Such formulations were not new; they developed as part of the biblical witness, as we have already seen in the text from 1 John quoted above. Similarly, the baptismal text was already evident at the end of Matthew's Gospel: "Go therefore and make disciples of all nations, baptizing them in the name of the Father and of the Son and of the Holy Spirit" (Mt 28:19).

The Truths of the Faith

Other formulations were even simpler and affirmed the faith of the church in Jesus as Lord and Savior, as the one put to death and raised up by God. Essentially these were statements that Jesus was the revelation of God and that in him the truth about God and God's promise for the whole of creation are known. Such formulations found their way into the preaching of the apostles and their writings to the newly formed Christian communities. Thus, for example, in the Pentecost speech (Acts 2:36), Peter proclaims:

> *Therefore let the entire house of Israel know with certainty that God has made him both Lord and Messiah, this Jesus whom you crucified.*

Paul gives a fuller statement when writing to the Corinthians (1 Cor 15:3–5):

> *For I handed on to you as of first importance what I in turn had received: that Christ died for our sins in accordance with the scriptures, and that he was buried, and that he was raised on the third day in accordance with the scriptures, and that he appeared to Cephas, then to the twelve.*

The letter to the Ephesians expresses it in terms of the mystery of God that has been finally and fully revealed in Jesus (Eph 1:8–10):

> *With all wisdom and insight [God] has made known to us the mystery of his will, according to his good pleasure that he set forth in Christ, as a plan for the fullness of time, to gather up all things in him, things in heaven and things on earth.*

Here the faith of the church is expressed in terms of the promise of God that has already begun in Christ. The author goes on to state that in Christ the dividing walls of hostility between peoples have been broken down. The challenge of belief in this God is then expressed in terms of reconciliation.

Throughout its history, the church has expressed its faith by means of formulations, the most solemn of which were defined in a conciliar act. Often these were necessary in order to avoid a distortion of the truth. They did not try to say all that could be said about the faith—that would be impossible—but they set boundaries for belief. The clearest example of such a formula is the Nicene Creed,[7] often referred to as the "Symbol of Faith."

The structure of the Nicene Creed is quite simple and has been formed around the affirmation that God is a Trinity. Hence there are three fundamental statements of the Christian faith in God: we believe in one God the Father, the Almighty; we believe in one Lord, Jesus Christ, the only Son of God; we believe in the Holy Spirit. Each of these statements goes on to make very specific affirmations about the particular person of the Trinity. For example, it is affirmed concerning the person of Jesus that he is "begotten, not made, of one being with the Father." This very careful formulation was intended to preserve the truth of the divinity of Christ in the face of the theological disputes of the fourth century. Built around these three fundamental affirmations is a series of statements that have come down to us as particular doctrines. When we look at the Nicene Creed, we will easily identify such doctrines as creation, redemption, the church, and the sacraments. We will also recognize a concern to speak of the promise made by God and consequent Christian hope.

Finding Language to Express the Faith

The creed that has come down to us was written in the language and thought forms of the fourth century. Since then, it has been a source of theological reflection as each generation has endeavored to interpret it and to keep its basic meaning alive in the Christian people. In chapter 5 we will consider the tools theology uses to interpret such faith expressions. We cannot avoid the search for appropriate language to express the faith (although such language will not usually take a credal form of expression). The task of the theologian is to work with words to express meaning.

From the earliest times in the church, it has been recognized that the faith can be expressed in a variety of ways, using different languages, concepts, and images. In the second century, Irenaeus (115–90), a theologian and bishop, noted that the diversity of places where the faith was experienced and lived would lead to a variety of ways of expressing the one faith. Nevertheless, he said, the faith was one:

> The Church, as we have said before, though disseminated throughout the whole world, carefully guards this preaching and this faith which she has received, as if she dwelt in one house. She likewise believes these things as if she had but one soul and one and the same heart; she preaches, teaches, and hands them down harmoniously, as if she possessed but one mouth. For, though the languages throughout the world are dissimilar, nevertheless the meaning of the tradition is one and the same. To explain, the churches founded in Germany do not believe or hand down any-

*thing else; neither do those founded in Spain or Gaul or Libya or
in the central regions of the world.*[8]

It is important to acknowledge two ideas in Irenaeus's formulation: first, that there is one faith and the unity of the faith is essential to its integrity, and second, that the diversity of places where that faith is lived means that there must be a diversity of expression. In the early church, it was unthinkable that there should be only one expression of faith. The church was aware that the unity of the faith would be quickly destroyed if it could not take root in a particular way in different places. Uniformity would, in fact, distort the truth of the faith and lead quickly to its being stifled as a vital force in the particular places and societies where it was taking root.

Creeds such as the Nicene Creed, although they utilize a classical language to express the faith, still need to be translated into the thought forms, idioms, and imagery of particular cultural groups. Karl Rahner has rightly made the claim that "the effective mission of the Church in the face of modern disbelief requires a testimony to the Christian message in which this message really becomes intelligible for people today."[9] He emphasizes the importance of finding formulations of the faith—he calls them short credal statements—that take account of a great range of diversity:

> We can say, therefore, that we may try to formulate many of these basic creedal statements of the faith. They can vary not only according to the differences of the nations, of cultural and historical areas, and of the world religions which co-determine a particular situation. They can also vary according to the social level, the age, and so on, of those to whom the basic creedal statement is directed.[10]

The unity of the faith, especially as it takes shape in words, is thus subject to some tension. An important role of the church is to provide a means of maintaining the unity of faith in the midst of such tension. From the time of the early church, conciliar structures were developed to respond to fundamental questions about the faith. Indeed, the great ecumenical councils have left us with precise dogmatic definitions and statements of doctrine. The most recent council, Vatican II (1962–65), reminded us that in dealing with the unity of the faith, we should bear in mind the notion of the *hierarchy of truths.*

Article 11 of *Unitatis Redintegratio,* the Decree on Ecumenism, noted that when dealing with doctrines there exists a "hierarchy" of truths "since they vary in their relation to the foundation of the Christian faith."

A useful image to explain what the council meant here is that of a sphere. We can imagine that the truths of the faith form this sphere and that the center or core of the sphere is what is referred to as the foundation of the faith. All doctrines are related to that foundation and both take their meaning from, and help to illuminate, the depth of meaning of the foundation. Let's take a simple example to illustrate this point: the decision of the Council of Ephesus in 431 to speak of Mary as the *Theotokos* (or God-bearer) was above all else an affirmation of the incarnation of Jesus. Mary is called the Mother of God because Jesus was truly God and truly human. This particular doctrine, then, is properly understood in relation to the foundation of the faith, namely the truth about Jesus as the self-revelation of God. Furthermore, it helps the believer appreciate the significance of that foundation.

One consequence of the notion of the hierarchy of truths is that greater weight can be placed on some doctrines than on others. This does not mean that some doctrines are dispensable. Presumably if they help to illuminate the foundation of the faith, they express the truth and cannot be denied or opposed. However, it does mean that not all Christians will place the same emphasis on all doctrines. Cultural and historical factors may well mean that certain doctrines are favored over others in expressing the foundation of the Christian faith in particular circumstances. In other words, the hierarchy of truths helps us deal with diversity in expressing the faith.

A further consequence of this notion is that particular groups develop their own "guiding symbol" that marks the pattern of their belief.[11] This becomes the lens through which they formulate words to express the faith and thus develop specific confessions of faith. It also determines other elements of Christian life, such as worship and witness. This becomes obvious when we look at the different churches and Christian communions. There are specific elements, for example, in Orthodoxy, Catholicism, Lutheranism, Anglicanism, or Calvinism that distinguish them from each other. They will all give different prominence, among other things, to the death of Jesus, to his resurrection, and to the Holy Spirit in the life of the church; yet they will all affirm the fundamental faith in these matters.[12]

It is therefore imperative that Christians be able to recognize the unity of the faith in its diverse expressions. In this way, the earlier statement that the faith is held in the community, in the church, becomes even more significant. One aspect of being the church is that the community in its various places and from its various perspectives and vantage points continually calls communities in other places and other contexts to a reflective profession of faith. The task of recognizing the faith professed by the other entails a challenge to recognize where our own word and witness are inadequate or incomplete. We are aware, for example, of the way liberation theology, which arises from particular cultural and social circumstances, has challenged people in other contexts to think about the meaning of the foundation of the faith and the way they give witness to it. Similarly, the experience and reflection of women has challenged, among other things, the language we use to speak of the self-revelation of God and to name God.

Conclusion

We began this chapter by speaking of the experience of faith. This idea has never been far from our view even as we have focused at other times on the content of faith. We have come to appreciate that the experience and the content of faith are intimately linked. To put it simply: both are concerned about aspects of naming our experience of God. Theology assists this process, for in doing theology we not only interpret the data of revelation, but we also find appropriate language to speak the truth about God. Throughout this chapter we have thus seen what it means to claim that theology is grounded in faith.

The history of Christianity, particularly the Reformation and Counter-Reformation, also makes us aware that these two aspects of faith can become separated from each other, with one aspect being emphasized at the expense of the other. When this happens, our statements about faith become incomplete. On the one hand, the content of faith, separated from the life of the believer and the believing community, becomes irrelevant to human life. On the other hand, the act of faith, separated from its content, becomes empty and totally subjective. Catholic theological reflection on the unity of the two aspects found clear expression in Vatican II's teaching in the Dogmatic Constitution on Divine Revelation, *Dei Verbum:*

"The obedience of faith" must be our response to God who reveals. By faith one freely commits oneself entirely to God, making "the full submission of intellect and will to God who reveals," and willingly assenting to the revelation given by God. For this faith to be accorded we need the grace of God, anticipating it and assisting it, as well as the interior helps of the Holy Spirit, who moves the heart and converts it to God, and opens the eyes of the mind and "makes it easy for all to accept and believe the truth." The same Holy Spirit constantly perfects faith by his gifts, so that revelation may be more and more deeply understood. (DV 5)

The perfecting of faith and the deepening of our understanding of revelation are ultimately about being in touch with the promise of God and its meaning in our existential situation. In the process of doing theology, we work this out in an intelligent way and thereby give account of our hope.

QUESTIONS FOR REFLECTION

1. How did you come to faith? What has challenged your faith? What has encouraged and supported your faith?

2. Is the faith response a reasonable one for a modern person?

3. What is the guiding symbol in your overall pattern of belief?

4. Prepare a short credal formula to express your faith.

SUGGESTIONS FOR FURTHER READING

- Haight, Roger. *Dynamics of Theology.* New York: Paulist Press, 1990.

- Kasper, Walter. *An Introduction to Christian Faith.* New York: Paulist Press, 1980.

- Kelly, Tony. *The Creed by Heart: Re-learning the Nicene Creed.* Blackburn: HarperCollinsReligious, 1996.

- Metz, Johannes Baptist and Edward Schillebeeckx, eds. *The Teaching Authority of Believers. Concilium* 180 (1985).

NOTES

[1]For example, Roger Haight, *Dynamics of Theology* (New York: Paulist Press, 1990), 32–48.

[2]Bernard J. Cooke, *The Distancing of God: The Ambiguity of Symbol in History and Theology* (Minneapolis: Fortress Press, 1990).

[3]St. Augustine, *Confessions*, tr. with an introduction and notes by Henry Chadwick (Oxford: Oxford University Press, 1991), 201.

[4]*St. Augustine: Tractates on the Gospel of John 11–27*, tr. John W. Rettig, The Fathers of the Church 79 (Washington: The Catholic University of America Press, 1988), tr. 26.4, p. 263.

[5]Notice how he has taken the Abraham story and begun to interpret it in the light of the Christian revelation.

[6]Herbert Vorgrimler, "From *Sensus Fidei* to *Consensus Fidelium*," in *The Teaching Authority of Believers,* ed. Johannes-Baptist Metz and Edward Schillebeeckx, *Concilium* 180 (1985), 8.

[7]The complex history of this creed need not detain us here. The creed formulated at the council of Nicaea in 325 was the basis for a more developed creed formulated at the Council of Constantinople in 381. Several centuries later the Western church acted unilaterally (that is, not in an ecumenical council) to add the phrase *filioque* (referring to the Holy Spirit proceeding from the Father *and the Son*) to the third article of the creed. It is this version that we refer to as the "Nicene Creed" and use in our liturgy.

[8]*St. Irenaeus of Lyons Against the Heresies* I,10,2, tr. and annotated by Dominic J. Unger with further revisions by John J. Dillon, Ancient Christian Writers 55 (New York: Paulist Press, 1992), 49.

[9]Karl Rahner, *Foundations of Christian Faith: An Introduction to the Idea of Christianity*, tr. William V. Dych (New York: Crossroad, 1982), 449.

[10]Rahner, *Foundations*, 452.

[11]Cf. Maurice Wiles, "What Christians Believe," in *The Oxford Illustrated History of Christianity*, ed. John McManners (Oxford: Oxford University Press, 1992), 567.

[12]Despite the centuries-long dispute between East and West about the Holy Spirit (related to the *filioque* clause), many theologians today would claim that there is still a common faith about this matter.

Chapter Four

ATTENTIVE TO THE WORD

> This chapter introduces readers to the historical and literary elements involved in the interpretation of the Bible. Theology uses this critical understanding of the Bible as one of its foundations.

Sometimes we hear it said that Christianity, with Judaism and like Islam, is a "religion of the book." As a way of depicting the sense of a shared inheritance among the three religions that acknowledge Abraham, such a statement is useful enough. It can be misleading, however, if we understand it to mean that Judaism and Christianity are based on the Bible, since the Bible is not really a source of either Jewish or Christian faith. Faith, as we have seen in the previous chapter, is not something that comes from a book. Faith is a personal experience, an attitude toward life, and a way of living that is rooted in a communal experience and expressed in a statement of faith or belief, a creed that is both personal and communal.

All of this means that if we were to give the Bible to someone and tell the person that he or she would find faith by reading it, we would be implying, erroneously, that the Bible has certain magical qualities that operate independently of a person's context and experience. Thus, the story of Augustine's conversion told in the previous chapter is not a story about the special powers of the Bible that enabled Augustine to find the answer to his struggles, but it is about how the word of God in the Bible connects with God's word spoken in the whole of Augustine's life.

If it were true that the Bible is a magical book, a book that contains the answers to any question we might ask, there would be no need for the interpretative and rational processes at the heart of theology. The truth, of course, is that the Bible cannot perform magic; however, this truth does not alter the fact that the Bible is crucial to the life of the Christian community.

In the Judaeo-Christian perspective, the Bible is an aspect of the tradition of faith. In this context, *tradition* includes two elements. The first is the actual process of transmission implied in the Latin word *tradere,* which means "to hand over." This is the handing over, from generation to generation, of what is a significant manifestation of the community's life, identity, and destiny: "When your children ask you in time to come, 'What is the meaning of these things that the Lord our God has commanded you?' then you shall say to your children..." (Dt 6:20–21). The second element is the content of the process: the stories, sayings, laws, and everything else that make up the tradition.

In the biblical world, therefore, tradition carries a positive meaning. It expresses the dynamic and enlivening handing on of what is precious for the community's self-understanding, values, and goals. Each moment in this process contributes its own gift to enrich and revitalize what is being handed on. In other words, biblical tradition is not mere repetition, but it also provides nourishment and energy. It is not simply about the past, but it is for the present and toward a future. Biblical tradition, therefore, no less than any of the aspects of the church's tradition referred to in previous chapters, cannot be separated from the work of the Holy Spirit in the church.

This chapter seeks to capture the richness of this biblical tradition. The chapter has three aims: to show why the Bible is a primary resource for the church and, therefore, for theology; to indicate something of the connection between the Bible and theology; and to show how the Bible can best be approached so that we can not only be enriched by it, but also resist the temptation to think of it as a magical book whose meaning can be gained without any effort on our part.

Although this book is primarily about theology rather than biblical studies, familiarity with the Bible and a knowledge of how to interpret the Bible are indispensable foundations for theology. This is particularly true in our current cultural climate where "fundamentalism"—the attitude that wants to exempt the Bible from any examination, that demands that every word of the Bible be accepted as God's direct dictation, that refuses to acknowledge that the Bible could contain any errors of fact or history, that denies to human beings the right to interpret the Bible, on the grounds that the Bible interprets itself for us—is so strong. In addition, a good understanding of the principles of biblical studies is beneficial because it can free us from the fear that has often been prevalent in Catholicism that study of the Bible is somehow dangerous and will undermine our faith.

This chapter will show that both fundamentalism and the fear of biblical studies are flawed, and that both do violence to the authentic ways in which the study of the scriptures can enhance our faith. Only when those attitudes are revealed as impoverished will it be possible to consider properly the relationship between the Bible and theology.

Our discussion of the Bible and of the use of the Bible in theology can best be understood as the attempt to answer a series of questions. Some of the key questions are: What is the Bible? What is special about the Bible? How did the Bible come to be? Why does the Bible need to be interpreted? How are we to interpret the Bible? Is there any difference between using the word *Bible,* and referring to the book by terms such as "scripture," "scriptures," "sacred scriptures," or "Word of God"? What is the relationship between the people of God, both Israel and the Christian church, and the Bible? How can the individual's personal reading of the Bible be integrated with this communal listening dimension? Is there an official interpretation of the Bible? These questions are at the heart of the next few pages.

What Is the Bible?

The first point that must be made is that the Bible is not a single theological composition. It is a library, a record that encompasses many generations, locations, and religious insights. The word *Bible* comes from the Greek word meaning "books." In theology, therefore, we approach the Bible not as an inspiring or devotional work, though it is that, but rather as the community's treasure-house from which it draws in order to reflect on and articulate itself and its mission. Second, the Bible is a vehicle that unveils God and God's will; its focus is the intersection of the divine and the human; its core is the story of the relationship between God and God's people. Though grounded in the human story, the truth of the Bible is not to be found in historical accuracy or scientific insight. Its truth is "that which God wanted put into the sacred writings for the sake of our salvation."[1] It is the fact that the Bible is the vehicle for this truth that constitutes the Bible as "the word of God." We may summarize this understanding of the Bible by a series of *R*s: the Bible is the **R**ecord of divine **R**evelation; it **R**emembers and **R**e-presents that Revelation; it thus elicits a **R**esponse from the hearer or reader.

The Bible recalls in order to celebrate. It is a dynamic, not a passionless, retelling of the community's story, one that both communicates and stimulates. To remember means more than simply "not forget" or "bring back to mind." Rather, it implies a positive act, keeping something (an event, a promise) before one's eyes as motivation or encouragement or challenge. "Remember your congregation" (Ps 74:2): Israel is calling on God to save her. "Remember the wonderful works he has done" (Ps 105:5): in this prayer of thanksgiving for God's past deeds, which become present again in the remembering, Israel is being summoned to repentance and a renewed future. "Remember me when you come into your kingdom" (Lk 23:42): the man beside Jesus on the cross is expressing hope and trust in him.

When we approach the biblical text as a source of theology, we recognize that in a number of ways the Bible is prophetic: it preserves the tradition of a God whose will is to save us, it unfolds that tradition in the story of Israel and the church, and it invites the community to live in faithfulness by that tradition as they listen to that story. It is neither a database of supernatural information nor a source book of solutions to religious questions.

The readers of this book probably bring a great range of previous experiences of the Bible—experiences that might have been negative as well as positive. Most of us also consider ourselves to be familiar with the Bible to a greater or lesser extent. With the steady development of, and interest in, biblical studies within the Catholic community, not only has the usage of the Bible increased, but the Bible has influenced individuals and groups in significant ways. Our reflections so far, however, have sought to alert us to the many dimensions of the Bible, dimensions that our familiarity with favorite texts, popular passages, and Bible stories may actually obscure for us. We hope that this chapter will help the reader to appreciate in a new way the richness of the Bible.

The Bible and the Influence of Culture

The scenery in films, news footage from Israel, and pictures of the world's ancient civilizations can all influence us subliminally as we read or listen to the Bible. As students of the Bible, we need to be aware of the impact of these factors, since they can be quite misleading. In order to appreciate the richness of the Bible, we need to understand something of the culture out of which the books of the Bible emerged and the processes involved in the production of the texts we have today. We need to recognize how different all of that is from our own time and culture.

The geographical world in which the Bible, especially the Old Testament, developed is usually known as the Middle East—a designation from the standpoint of Greece and Rome. Any contemporary atlas of the Bible will point out the land masses, the major river systems, the climate, and other important features of the area that was home to the events described in the Bible. It was a world of shifting populations, of immense creativity in agriculture, art, writing, and social and religious structures. The literature of the Old Testament is rooted in a Semitic world that expressed itself in mythology, epic narratives, and concepts such as divine kingship and the kingdom of God.

Though the world in which the New Testament developed inherited much of the earlier culture, it had its own distinctive features of language, imagery, and conceptual framework. This we may describe as the Graeco-Roman world, which manifests its own particular features, as well as important similarities with the Semitic culture that was home to the people of Israel, whose experience of God is recorded in the Bible. Our own culture, in turn, though it inherits much from the ancient cultures of the biblical world, is vastly different. Bridging these gaps is vital in the process of understanding and interpreting the biblical text. One key plank of this bridge is the recognition of the difference between the aural cultures which produced the Bible and the written and visual culture in which we live.

Our culture, a culture in which television and video screens proliferate, is predominantly a visual one. Texts and pictures, singly or jointly, are our principal means of communication. More and more technologically sophisticated means of visual communication are at our disposal. Speakers and teachers, stand-up comedians, and rock bands need to gain and retain our attention by their visual techniques as well as by their oral techniques—what they say or sing. The world in which the Bible developed, however, was predominantly an aural culture. Listening, rather than reading, was its basis. Dancing, drawing, and drama complemented, but did not displace, telling stories, reciting poems, and singing songs. This form of communicating can be very intense and involving. Have you ever noticed how a group of attentive youngsters, gathered around a good storyteller, tend to lean in toward the storyteller? This is the style in which Semitic cultures transmitted the stories that were constitutive of their identity.

This fact means that our modern understanding of authorship is inappropriate when we come to the writing in the Bible. Only a few books of the Bible, Paul's letters, for example, were written by one person as that person's own composition. It is more usual that the biblical author was the final person in a long chain of tradition, the person who wrote from within the community as its servant. Therefore, interpreting the Bible requires that we do more than simply decipher the words on the page. We must enter into a world in which the words on the page both disclose and conceal meaning.

The library of the Bible is a collection whose books are written in Hebrew, Aramaic, and Greek. The fact that the Bible is written in these ancient languages should alert us to the fact that its meaning will not automatically be clear for us who are accustomed to the vocabulary and style of contemporary English. We need to recognize that we are all dependent on language and that language evolves. This fact means that a study of the history of words and grammar can enrich our appreciation of the Bible, just as a study of the English used in the time of Shakespeare can enhance our enjoyment of *Romeo and Juliet.* Even more fundamentally, however, we need to appreciate that the books of the Bible as we have them today are the product of a long history that began long before any words were written down. In order to appreciate the richness of the Bible, we need, therefore, to acknowledge the differences between the world of the Bible and our world.

Our word *scriptures,* which simply means "writings," may obscure some of these fundamental cultural differences. Obviously, the oral or word-of-mouth traditions were eventually committed to writing; these traditions were assembled and edited into what we call a "book" of the Bible. These various books were ultimately assembled into a collection, accepted within the community as its own, to which the term *canon* is often applied. However, this was the end of a very long process involving centuries of the community's life.

The texts we possess today are the product of the dynamic and enlivening handing on—tradition—of what is precious for the community's self-understanding, values, and goals. Each moment in this process of handing on contributed its own gift to enrich and revitalize the content of the tradition. Thus, the tradition that was ultimately expressed in the written texts of the Bible was not mere repetition, but was what had nourished and energized the community's faith. The Bible's place in the Christian community today derives from the fact that it continues to nourish and energize that community: the Bible continues to be a source of encounter with God's Spirit.

Our models and patterns of imagining and thinking about the Bible are inevitably influenced by our own culture and worldview. We are probably all familiar with illustrations depicting "biblical writers" seated at their desks, quill in hand, eyes raised to the heavens as they compose a book of the Bible, possibly with the Holy Spirit or an angel overseeing the work. Such a picture affirms the truth that the Bible is a special kind of book, but at the same time it falsifies the way biblical tradition and inspiration work. As was discussed in the previous chapter, the "word of God" is not something extrinsic, not something that is spoken into a historical vacuum; but it is the term used by individuals and, most importantly, by communities, to describe their sense of God's self-communication, which is inseparable from their history and their culture.

In order to enter into the world of the Bible, to interpret the biblical texts, and to value their authentic meaning and relevance, we need to be aware of the cultural aspects we have discussed above. This means that we approach the books of the Bible with careful attentiveness, respecting their structures and modes of communication, rather than imposing our own categories on them.

The Books of the Bible

"I will make a new covenant with the house of Israel" (Jer 31:31). The notion of *covenant* is crucial for understanding the content of the Bible. Used in the Old Testament to describe the relationship between God and Israel, it came to be used by the early Christian community to describe its relationship to God in Jesus Christ. The early Christian community also applied the word to its growing collection of writings that were being used in worship and instruction. Inevitably, the writings of the Jewish community were called the "old" covenant. We are accustomed to the term *testament,* which comes from the Latin translation of the Greek word for covenant. Of course, Jesus and his immediate followers knew no such distinction. So when Paul asserts that Jesus "was raised on the third day according to the scriptures," he was referring to the scriptures of Judaism, not the New Testament.

The early Christian community did not see itself as initiating a new set of sacred scriptures in opposition to those it had inherited from Judaism. A number of factors, including the fall of Jerusalem in 70 C.E., the separation of Christianity from Judaism, and the teaching of Marcion (died 160), who proposed rejecting the scriptures of Judaism because Christianity had nothing in common with Judaism, seem to have contributed to the development of a set of scriptures that included both the scriptures of Judaism and certain Christian writings, notably the Gospels and the letters of Paul.

At the end of the first century of the Common Era (C.E.), *scriptures* was a fluid term within Judaism. This can be seen from the fact that the Septuagint, the earliest version of the Old Testament in Greek, consisted not only of the Greek translation of the Hebrew books, but also included some books not found in the Hebrew Bible, books that later came to be called "apocryphal" or "deuterocanonical." Many of the Old Testament quotations found in New Testament writings are from the Septuagint, which seems to suggest that it was the Greek text, not the Hebrew text, that comprised the scriptures for the early church.

In 1546 the Catholic Church at the Council of Trent defined the canon of the Old and the New Testaments. Trent opposed the claims of some of the Reformers that the Old Testament canon consisted only of the books in the Hebrew Bible. Thus, though the major Christian churches accept the same books of the New Testament canon, they still differ on the books of the Old Testament canon. Contemporary English versions will indicate the larger (Catholic) list by a comment such as "including the deuterocanonical or apocryphal books."[2]

At this point it would be useful to consult your Bible's table of contents and check the names and arrangement of the books of the Bible. The Catholic Old Testament contains forty-six books, divided into Pentateuch (5), historical books (16), wisdom and poetry books (7), and books of the prophets (18). The Catholic New Testament contains twenty-seven books, divided into Gospels (4), historical book (1), Pauline and other letters (14), catholic letters (7), and an apocalyptic book (1).

The Bible, as we have noted, is best recognized as a collection of collections of collections. In other words, with few exceptions, each book of the Bible is itself the fruit of many human hands, not to mention many vicissitudes. Moreover, we can also recognize that the books themselves may be grouped together. From the beginning, the first five books of the Old Testament seem to have gained a position of preeminence within the Israelite/Jewish community. Known as the *Torah* (or Teaching), they are the books of Genesis, Exodus, Leviticus, Numbers, and Deuteronomy. Many allusions to this collection are found in the New Testament, for example: "Do not think I have come to abolish the law *[Torah]* or the prophets" (Mt 5:17). A second collection, a kind of commentary on the Torah, is called the Prophets and includes both historical and oracular writings. These are prophetic in the sense that they are theological judgments on Israel's living as God's covenanted people in conformity with the Torah. A third collection is composed of the Psalms and the Wisdom writings, together with a few books not easily categorized. We find this threefold division referred to in the New Testament: "Everything written about me in the law of Moses, the prophets, and the psalms must be fulfilled" (Lk 24:44).

In the New Testament we are also accustomed to collections, traditionally known as the Gospels and the Epistles (or Letters). This, however, is not a very satisfactory division, since the Gospel of John is a quite distinctive work of literature compared with the Synoptic Gospels of Matthew, Mark, Luke. The Gospel of Luke and the Acts of the Apostles form a unified work, and to separate them does not do justice to the work as a whole.

The Bible and History

Dates and places in the biblical record have fascinated its readers over the generations. This fascination has given rise to questions: When was a particular book written? When did a particular event in the passage take place? Where did it happen? Because reconstruction of the past forms an important element in our historical understanding, these kinds of questions can often assume major importance when addressed to the Bible. At the outset, we offer two preliminary observations. First, in keeping with what was said earlier, the Bible is not history; it does not purport to present us with the facts of the past for our information or our edification, nor even to speak of the past in an objective way. Second, to know something of the historical, social, geographical, and cultural setting of a biblical text enables us to enter effectively into its frame of reference and therefore to understand it better. Entry into the text's frame of reference, however, is not an exercise in ancient history, since our focus is the biblical text itself. The biblical material can only be used very cautiously as a source for historical reconstruction.

We may note an important issue involved in our reflection at this point. It is useful to distinguish between two historical worlds when we are studying the Bible. First, there is the internal world of a particular biblical text (a passage or a whole book) and the context or setting that is explicitly or implicitly presumed in the text and that gives shape and expression to that text. Second, there is the external world in which the Bible developed, the world of the Middle East, of Greece, and of Rome. This is the actual context—historical, geographical, cultural, and religious—in which the biblical traditions, both oral and written, were formed and assembled, and in which the canon of the Bible came to be established. We can come to know this world through the study of archaeology and history, using the contemporary sources available to us, such as items uncovered by archaeological excavation (ranging from burial practices to pottery, from tools to towns), inscriptions, literary documents, business records, and historical archives. Sometimes, of course, these two historical worlds may overlap, but it is important to recognize their distinctive contribution.

The book of Deuteronomy, for example, presents itself as a series of extended addresses by Moses to the people of Israel, camped on the eastern side of the river Jordan and about to enter the land of Canaan. This is the world of the text. However, from close analysis of the book, it becomes clear that the world the book actually addresses is very different. It is the world of the seventh and sixth centuries B.C.E., in which Israel is being called to repentance and reformation as it faces the crisis of invasion and destruction by the armies of the Mesopotamian empires of Assyria and Babylon. Our present task is to explore further this second consideration, because it is in the light of this background of the historical dimension that the detailed study of particular texts takes place.

The Historical Background of the Bible

Three historical moments may be distinguished when we examine the history of the development of the biblical text. The first is the establishment of the people of Israel in the early centuries after the beginning of the first millennium B.C.E. (900 and onwards). This was the context in which the traditions of the various groups began to come together in order to express this people's newfound sense of identity and destiny. The story of the dynasty founded on David provided a means of communicating this vision and faith, as well as a symbol to embody it. What came to be preserved was dictated by the particular demands of Israel's self-understanding. It addressed questions of vital importance for Israel's continuing life: Who was their God? What was the will of God?

The second critical moment was at the beginning of the sixth century B.C.E. (587), when the city of Jerusalem and the temple were razed by the Babylonian armies of Nebuchadnezzar and large numbers of the Israelites were taken off into exile. More than a hundred and thirty years before this event, a similar fate had befallen the city of Samaria at the hands of the Assyrian armies of Shalmaneser and Sargon. In the context of such a calamity, Israel was impelled to reflect again on its story over the previous centuries—the traditions, oral and written, that were its heritage—and shape it anew in this utterly new situation. The story is recorded, not for its own inherent historical interest, but to shed light on Israel's present and to offer hope for its future. The Abraham narratives, which are the product of this period, are not archival relics from which a distant past might be constructed, but are an affirmation of Israel's trust in the divine will, a trust that persisted despite the darkness. Something of the flavor of this perspective may be seen in a little Jewish poem discovered in a cellar in Cologne at the end of the Second World War:

> *I believe in the sun even when it is not shining,*
> *I believe in God even when God is silent.*

The third critical moment came at the end of the first century C.E. (from 70 onwards) with the destruction of Jerusalem and the temple by the Roman armies. Caught up in this were both Judaism and the newly emerging Christianity. As well, the Christian community was now seeing the death of its first members. Once again, catastrophe on this huge scale impelled both religious communities, Jewish and Christian, to examine their respective traditions as well as their relationship. As far as the Bible was concerned, they began to ask: What is to be accepted as "sacred scriptures"? How were the traditions to be expressed and passed on so that the community might be able to make sense of the present and move forward to the future? What writings were to be excluded or relegated to secondary status? This process we know as the development of the canon of scripture. Christianity and Judaism set out on their own paths, expressed in the different collections of scriptures designated as sacred. The separation into the Old and the New Testaments had begun.

This reflection enables us to understand the Bible dynamically; that is, not as the work of writers in the quiet of a study, but as the response to momentous religious, social, and political upheavals, in the light of which the community sought to draw together its traditions, oral and written, in order to define itself and its destiny. Thus, wherever a biblical narrative is situated—historically, geographically, and sociologically—its primary focus is not authentic reproduction of history, geography, or sociology, but religious insight, theological sensitivity, and the human-divine encounter. When our study of the Bible attempts to discover the historical background to the Bible, its aim is to make sense of the biblical text, not to use it to write ancient history.

The Use of the Bible in Theology

Unless we have a well-developed understanding of the nature of the Bible and a grasp of how to interpret it, we will be likely to misuse the Bible in theology. A failure to respect the nature and purpose of the Bible might reveal itself, for example, in the use of "proof texts" as a theological method. Proof texts are quotes from the scriptures, used without reference to the original purpose or setting of the text, to "prove" that the Bible supports a claim that is itself not derived from the Bible. An example of this flawed approach would be the use of quotes from the book of Revelation, one of the most poetic and figurative books of the New Testament, to prove not only that the world will be obliterated by a nuclear holocaust, but also that the number of survivors has been determined in advance by God.

When we turn to the authentic use of the Bible in theology, we see that there is no one method that is mandatory for all theologians. Above all else, we need to remember that theology is not simply a commentary on the scriptures, and that the theologian, as was discussed in chapter 1, makes use, not just of the Bible, but of the church's whole heritage of faith as well as the insights of the human sciences. Nonetheless, it is true that theology depends on the Bible. How, then, is the Bible essential for theology? This question is answered in a succinct manner by the contemporary American theologian Roger Haight, who describes the Bible as both a negative and a positive norm for theology.

According to Haight, the Bible is a negative norm in that theology, if it seeks to be authentic to the faith of the Christian community, cannot manufacture a god who is positively at odds with the portrayal of God in the scriptures. Thus, for example, a theologian who argued that God is either impersonal or demonic would, in fact, be operating outside the faith of the Christian community. On the other hand, the Bible operates as a positive norm for theology, argues Haight, in that it guides and shapes the person of the theologian.[3] In other words, if theology, as was argued in chapter 1, takes place within a community of faith, then the fact that the Bible is a primary influence on that community of faith means that the Bible is also a primary influence on the theologians who operate within the community. In translating the tradition of faith into the context of the present, the theologian must be faithful to the God revealed in the scriptures, for it is that God who is at the heart of the community's life.

We have already seen in both chapters 1 and 3 that arriving at an expression of the church's faith involves the interplay of the community's "sense," guided by the Holy Spirit, of what is reconcilable with its faith and the judgment of the teaching authority, which is also guided by the Spirit. The church's sense of its faith is not, however, something magical; it is not something that operates independently of human efforts to understand the meaning and consequences of God's self-revelation, which is the foundation of the church. This fact becomes particularly clear when we explore it in relation to the Bible. Accordingly, what we will do in the remainder of this chapter is to enter into the world of *hermeneutics,* the science of interpretation. We will examine why the Bible needs to be interpreted, what methods of interpretation there are, and what results these methods produce.

The Necessity and Possibility of Interpretation

We have already seen in the first part of this chapter that the cultural differences between the world of the Bible and our world mean that we cannot assume that for us the meaning of a biblical text will always be transparent. In this section we will be concerned with the challenges raised for biblical studies by the differences in literary methods between the world of the Bible and our world.

Although its etymology is uncertain, it is most likely that the word *hermeneutics* comes from a Greek word that means, most generally, "interpretation." We can, however, nuance the theme of interpretation in three ways: first, it refers to attempts to communicate human thoughts by means of language, spoken and written; second, it refers to attempts to transfer or to translate the meaning from one language and culture into another; and third, it refers to attempts to explain the meaning of a particular text. In biblical studies, this is usually called *exegesis.*

Despite this arsenal of terms to describe interpretation, we might wonder whether the differences between the biblical culture and our own may be so vast that any efforts at translation are doomed to failure. In other words, we might wonder whether the Bible can be approached only as an interesting historical relic, but not as a text that can speak to our lives today. These concerns can be addressed from two angles: the notion of a "classic" in literary theory, and the place of the Bible in the life of the church.

A "classic" is a text whose meaning is not confined to the time and culture in which it was produced. Classic texts have what is often called an "excess of meaning" that allows them to speak to people in radically different cultures. For example, Homer's *Odyssey* and Shakespeare's *Macbeth* can challenge how we live today, even though their original context might seem alien to us. However, the fact that classic texts come from a different culture does make it necessary that they be interpreted. A classic is able to sustain different forms of interpretation, and this contributes to its ongoing life. Ultimately, what makes a literary work into a classic is that its themes are not time-conditioned.[4]

The notion of a classic did not arise out of a specifically Christian, or even a religious milieu, but it would be difficult to argue against the claim that the Bible is a classic. Not only has the Bible continued to influence people far removed from the context in which it was produced, but its theme centers on being human. Indeed, the figure of

Jesus is accessible to people because he is a human being whose message—love of God and love of neighbor—does not depend on any particular culture to make it comprehensible.

The notion of the classic is valuable not only because it provides a
vehicle for dialogue with those who might wonder about the use of the
Bible in the Christian community, but also because it reinforces the need
for interpretation of the Bible if we are to appropriate its meaning for
today. Ultimately, however, the place of the Bible in the church is derived
not from literary theory, but from the church's faith that the Bible is the
means for an ongoing encounter between God and ourselves:

> *The scriptures gather together, sum up and propose publicly in a*
> *written form the paradigmatic expression of the inner faith-life*
> *that constitutes the Christian Church.*[5]

Faith and the Interpretation of the Bible

To read and interpret the scriptures in faith does not require that
we possess a decoding device. If it did, it would imply that God has
encrypted a special message in the text that can be read only when we
see through the surface meaning to what is "behind" it. If we are seeking God's word in the scriptures, the primary task is to understand the
text we have in front of us.

Biblical interpretation in the church, therefore, can never bypass,
or dispense with, what is usually referred to as the *literal sense* of the
biblical text, a technical term that refers to the meaning the original
author intended to convey.[6] This literal sense is our customary way of
interpreting any text, spoken or written; it recognizes that a text is
something objective, that while we might interpret it, we do not construct it. It is vital to emphasize here that when it is applied to the Bible,
the literal sense is very different from a fundamentalist reading of the
biblical text that rejects scientific methods of interpretation and does
not take into consideration the original context of text and author.

The interpretation of the Bible within the church, however, is
never simply a neutral or technical act, but is guided by the belief that
the biblical text is the medium for God's self-revelation. This is the
conviction that the text has a *more-than-literal sense*. The fact that the
interpretation of the Bible in the church is seen as aiding the faith community's encounter with God expresses the church's belief that the

Holy Spirit who inspired the writers of the text is the same Spirit who inspires those who read the text in faith. This belief is grounded in the church's recognition that the biblical text was produced by the community as an expression of its faith that God's self-communication was for all people and all times. In other words, interpretation of the Bible in the church is about allowing the complete message of the Bible— God's word of self-revelation—to be heard, a message that can be heard only if the Bible is read and interpreted in faith, just as it was composed in faith. The members of the church, therefore, do not see less of the Bible than the disinterested critic, but claim to see more because of their faith that the biblical text provides a vehicle for the human encounter with God.

This encounter with God, however, is inseparable from an encounter with the text and from the meaning of the text, which is accessible to all. In turn, this means that the interpretation of the Bible within the church must be no less scientific or thorough than that undertaken by the person who approaches the Bible only as an interesting ancient text. Indeed, the church's faith would not be authentic if the church resisted the use of all possible means of approaching the Bible.

Finding the Meaning of Scripture

In seeking the literal sense, we need to remember the following factors. First, once a text is written down, later generations can add to it or subtract from it in the course of its transmission. This is called *redaction* or editing, and the person or persons who rework the text are called *redactors* or editors. The fact that texts undergo a whole process of addition and subtraction in the process of their formation means that we cannot know everything about the text if we simply read the words on the page as we have them now.

Second, the possibility that a text has been edited means that the written text has to be approached with a number of questions, such as: Why was a particular word used to describe an event? Did the original speaker use this or that particular word, or is it the scribe's expression, and hence an interpretation of the original speaker? Did Jesus actually say the words attributed to him by the Gospel writers, or are later authors theologizing, reflecting on Jesus' words from the perspective of the Christian church?

Third, words have different meanings according to different contexts. If, for example, someone says "I paid a high price for it" and we know that the context is that person's purchase of a new car, we interpret the statement to mean that the car was expensive. If, however, we know that the statement was made by a person who has revealed some corrupt practices, then we interpret the statement to mean that the person has been victimized in some way, such as by loss of employment, because of the revelations that were made. Hence, the literal sense itself may be figurative or metaphorical. This fact reinforces the importance of avoiding a fundamentalist interpretation that insists that the words on the page can mean only one thing. If we do not engage in the search for the literal sense, then we fall into *eisegesis,* reading into the text a meaning not intended by the author.

Fourth, to discover this literal sense, we need the sort of background information that we identified in the first part of this chapter. We need to know about the geography of biblical lands and about the knowledge gained by biblical archaeology; we need historical knowledge so as to be able to situate the biblical texts in their historical context; we need linguistic knowledge in order to understand the grammar, syntax, historical development, and meaning of the biblical languages, thereby enabling us to interpret the thought patterns of the authors who used these languages.

Fifth, the fact that our modern printed Bible is a text that has been passed down the generations through copyists and that has come down to us in thousands of manuscripts, ranging from complete copies of the Bible to fragments of a biblical text containing only a few words, raises questions about whether the text we have is the "real" text of the Bible. Obviously, we have no "autograph" or "original" version of the Bible, but by carefully sifting and comparing Hebrew or Greek manuscripts and the early translations such as Syriac and Latin, textual study of the Bible seeks to establish the most accurate version possible.

Methods of Interpretation

Window or Historical-Critical Methods

Various methods have been developed since the nineteenth century to respond to all these needs. Taken together, these methods, called *historical-critical* methods, provide the basis of all modern scientific analysis of the Bible. The historical-critical approach "opens up to the modern reader a path to the meaning of the biblical text, such as we have it today."[7] The three major critical approaches in the historical-critical method are source criticism, form criticism, and redaction criticism. These three approaches, which we will examine below, all treat the biblical text as a window through which one might look in order to find the original author or redactor's intention in writing down these particular words in this particular way.

SOURCE CRITICISM

Source criticism tries to discover the written sources that go to make up a text. It is interested in how an author composed a text, a chronology of the works involved in such an undertaking, the relationships between the various sources, and the theological ideas behind the sources used. In examining a text in this way, we ask questions of the text, such as: Does the author use one or more sources in this composition? What are the sources used? Have the sources been modified in any way by the author?

Various criteria have been developed to aid the source critic in answering the above questions. Some of the aspects of the biblical text that indicate the presence of different sources are repetitions and parallel passages, different theological language that utilizes unique vocabulary, stylistic changes, and apparent abrupt shifts from one idea to another or awkward connections that do not allow the text to flow smoothly. A useful working hypothesis is that no matter how careful an author is, that author is somehow bound to reproduce or reflect the sources used.[8]

Two of the major results of source criticism are the *documentary hypothesis* and the *two-source theory*. The *documentary hypothesis* refers to the notion that the Pentateuch, the Greek name for the first five books of the Old Testament, contains four main sources, each with a distinctive style and point of view: *J* or the *Jahwist* source offers the perspective of the Davidic court; *E* or the *Elohist* source has a perspective that comes from the northern kingdom of Israel and is sometimes anti-monarchist; *D* or the *Deuteronomist* source comes from a later time in the history of Israel and is guided by a desire for the reform of the people's religious practice; and *P* or the *Priestly* source writes after the exile of the people of Israel to Babylon and is concerned with matters relating to genealogies, laws, and regulations. These sources were combined at various stages in the history of the people of Israel to form our present text of the Pentateuch.

The *two-source theory* refers to the hypothesis that the Synoptic Gospels (Matthew, Mark, and Luke) have two major sources for their material about Jesus: the Gospel of Mark, and a collection of the sayings of Jesus used in the Gospels of Matthew and Luke but not in the Gospel of Mark. This source is commonly known as *Q,* which stands for the German word *Quelle,* which means "source."

FORM CRITICISM

Form criticism follows logically from source criticism. It is based on the conviction that the various sources reflected different oral and literary forms or genres that have their own histories. Form criticism investigates the history of the oral and literary forms that are at the basis of the sources.

Form criticism reflects the fact that human beings communicate via known patterns or forms, both verbal and written. Thus, a bank account balance sheet is a different form of communication from a letter; and within the form of letters, there are various types: business letters, love letters, "Dear John" letters, and so on. For communication to occur, the listener or reader must understand the pattern or form of communication chosen by the speaker/writer. For example, the humor contained in a pun or in irony will not be appreciated by someone who believes that humor must be packaged in the form of a joke with an identifiable punch line. Similarly, the beauty of John Keats's "Ode to a Grecian Urn" will not be appreciated by someone looking for a technical analysis of ancient ceramics. For those who study the literary forms of biblical literature, there is an even greater need to understand and appreciate the forms chosen and used by the biblical authors, so that the communication intended may be achieved.

Form criticism has helped us to recognize the many literary genres in the Bible, for example, proverbs, parables, folk stories, hymns, and laws. Form criticism has also made us aware that these literary forms have a written and an oral history behind their incorporation into the Bible. This allows us to understand the variants in the Bible: the two creation stories, the two flood stories, the three Synoptic Gospels, and the differing accounts of the Last Supper in the Gospels and in Paul. Furthermore, we recognize that the written and oral forms have a different

Sitz im Leben or "setting-in-life." That is, each stage of the formation of the text of the Bible has its own social situation that must be considered when we interpret a text.

REDACTION CRITICISM

Form criticism has its focus on the individual units within a biblical book rather than on the whole of the document. *Redaction criticism,* on the other hand, has as its focus the editorial process. Accepting the use of written sources and the various forms behind them, this critical approach tries to discern the theological tendencies of the final hand or redactor of the biblical texts.

Redaction criticism examines why certain sections of traditional material were selected for incorporation into the text and, indeed, why certain parts were omitted. Other questions that might interest the redaction critic are: What modifications seem to have been made to the sources? Why did the author or redactor arrange the final text in a particular way? Are there any original contributions from the author or redactor that appear to have no prehistory, whether written or oral?

Various occurrences in the biblical text highlight editorial activity. These are usually apparent in the Hebrew or Greek texts, but not so clear in translation. Sometimes the grammar is incorrect or elements that should be together are separated by a phrase that appears to be inserted. At other times a developed structural pattern is broken. In Matthew 5:21–48, for example, verse 31 breaks the pattern of verses 21, 27, 33, 38, and 48; in the other verses, Jesus begins with the words "You have heard that it was said," but verse 31 has "It is also said." There are many other examples, not the least among which are *doublets:* the occurrence twice of the same story, often with different theological emphases, such as the feeding of the five and four thousand in Mark 6:30–40 and Mark 8:1–10 respectively. In such instances, it appears that editors were unable to choose which version of the story to keep and so placed both in the text.

Mirror Methods

Since the 1960s, a paradigm shift or change of models has allowed new ways of approaching the biblical text:

> *Today, biblical scholarship is undergoing a shift in methodological emphasis toward an appreciation of the texts themselves as literary*

production in reaction to the dominant scholarly preoccupation with
the historical events behind the texts. This also involves a greater
awareness of the role of the reader in the art of interpretation.[9]

This development is described as a move from seeing the text through a "window" to seeing it through a "mirror." As we have seen, the "window" methods regarded the text as something through which the reader looked in order to discover what was originally said or the event that once took place. Today, the text is regarded not simply as a window, but also as a mirror; that is, the primary emphasis is not on the historical events on which the text might be based, but on how the plot, characters, values, and so on are understood now. Thus, the reader has become far more significant to the process of interpretation. Today it is recognized that in reading a text, a multiplicity of meanings may be understood. Depending on one's situation in life and the circumstances of the reading process, many different meanings can be discovered in the text; and all of them may be valid messages for the readers.

Although there are many more expressions of the mirror method than there are of the historical-critical method, certain ones are particularly beneficial to the student of theology. The approaches examined below all fall into the category of reader-oriented approaches. As such, they are more concerned with the reading process and the polyvalent meanings that arise when the reader reads the text.

LITERARY APPROACH

The *literary approach* examines the Bible as literature, using the tools and procedures of modern *literary criticism*. Key elements in this approach are *poetics* (the interpretation of poetical language) and *narrative analysis* (the interpretation of narrative or story texts). Both are very important for the student of the Bible, since much of our biblical literature is either poetry or narrative.

Narrative analysis examines the stories of the Bible by means of both ancient and modern methods of analyzing a story. Plot, time, characterization, narrator and reader, dialogue, and irony are some of the important elements in narrative criticism. These enable the reader of the biblical text to give new meaning to the words and ideas in the reading process. This is something beyond the author's/redactor's control; it brings the reader into the world of the text now, rather than the world of the author/redactor in the past.

We can illustrate the difference between these approaches by an examination of John's chapter on the Samaritan women at the well (Jn 4:4–42). Whereas a historical-critical reading of this text will strive to discover the historical Jesus behind the text, a narrative approach is not interested in this human Jesus of history, but rather with Jesus as the actor within the narrative.

A historical-critical reading of John 4:4–42 may examine the historical background surrounding Jews and Samaritans and highlight the fact that Jesus is being quite radical in speaking with a Samaritan, whom the Jews considered nonpersons. On the other hand, a mirror approach correctly and necessarily focuses on the understanding of the words themselves and the concepts behind them; this focus aids that part of the hermeneutical package called *translation.* By becoming part of the narrative of the text via the reading process, the reader can relate to Jesus in a much more active and personal way than through historical examination. The scene comes alive: the woman's gradual recognition of Jesus as Messiah is mirrored in our own lives, as we recognize Jesus as Lord.

RHETORICAL APPROACH

Underlying *rhetorical analysis* is the conviction that the biblical text is trying to persuade the reader to a particular point of view or to a particular action; as such, it is rhetorical. Rhetorical analysis can be divided into two approaches: the first is more traditional and is correctly part of the window approach to interpretation—an examination of texts from the standpoint of ancient Semitic or ancient Graeco-Roman rhetorical rules, thereby determining how and why the authors constructed the texts. Saint Paul, for example, is a master at using the tools of rhetoric, and an understanding of the rules of ancient rhetoric can help the student comprehend the arguments of Paul in his letters.

The second approach is more contemporary and overtly reader oriented. It asks questions such as: How does the Bible, the final text we possess today, influence my actions now? What does this text persuade me to do? This latter approach, often called the "new rhetoric," examines the way the Bible persuades and convinces.

"In the act of interpretation one does not just understand and comprehend texts and symbols,...but one also produces new meanings by interacting with them."[10] Such an approach is no longer neutral—that is, purely scientific or objective—without personal involvement.

Rather, every reading results in consequences for the life and belief of the person reading the text, and these will change in every rereading.

A historical-critical reading of the story about the queen and the child in Revelation 12 shows the basis of the story to be the common Mediterranean myth about a goddess and her god-child, such as Roma and Apollo the sun god. Furthermore, the symbolism contrasts the woman, the symbol of the New Jerusalem, the bride of Christ, with the evil city of Babylon, considered a great whore. A contemporary rhetorical reading examines the language in the text and shows that it conveys the idea that men's desire for power is justified on the grounds that such power is redirected to positive values, but when a woman wants power, she is called a "whore" and must be destroyed. Furthermore, the only positive image of woman in Revelation is the bride of the Lamb, who is praised for her silent, passive, powerless, sexually controlled, and pure approach to life.[11] The fact that the text can be read in a way that produces such a distorted view of women presents theology with a problem it must face if it is to relate the scriptures to our contemporary context, which is sensitive to any diminishment of the status and role of women in the world. A theological response to this challenge can be seen in the next method of exegesis that we will examine.

ADVOCACY EXEGESIS OR CONTEXTUAL APPROACHES

Contextual methods take into consideration the mind-set and the concerns of the readers. The two most prominent forms of this approach are the liberationist and the feminist.

The *liberationist* approach not only reads the text in the light of the principles of liberation theology but also seeks to understand the message of liberation in the text for today. Since it is reader oriented, the liberationist method "practices a reading of the Bible which is oriented to the needs of the people, who seek in the Scriptures nourishment for their faith and life."[12] This contextual approach focuses on what the text has to say to contemporary situations of oppression, inequality, injustice, and so on. The Bible is seen as offering spiritual nourishment for people engaged in a struggle for justice and freedom.

The story of the exodus in the Old Testament is a key text for the liberationist exegete. As God delivered the people of Israel from oppression and slavery in Egypt, so God will deliver God's people today from all forms of exploitation. This message of liberation speaks loudly to those suffering injustice, and the reading of the exodus story encourages action. The *Magnificat* (Lk 1:46–55) or Song of Mary also speaks volumes to those struggling for justice when it is read: "[God] has brought down the powerful from their thrones, and lifted up the lowly; he has filled the hungry with good things, and sent the rich away empty."

The result of this reading process is a Christian praxis that will lead to the transformation of society, bringing about the kingdom of God on earth. The Pontifical Biblical Commission's document *The Interpretation of the Bible in the Church* identifies two main principles behind this approach: first, God is the saving God of the poor, who "cannot tolerate injustice or oppression"; and second, exegesis must be involved in this salvific process of bringing liberation to the *anawim* or "little ones" of the Lord. Thus, exegesis, the interpretation of the biblical text, must be done within the context of the Christian community, because the Bible is God's liberating word for God's people.

The *feminist* approach reads the biblical text from the standpoint of women, discovering the richness of women's experience in the biblical text and translating this richness into the conditions of today's world. The feminist approach is a subset of the liberationist method; it seeks new insights into the role of women in the story of salvation and applies them to the role of women in contemporary culture. Feminist hermeneutics offers to the Christian community women's experience of God and the church, an experience that has been undervalued for most of the church's history.

Two key terms that must be appreciated when reading feminist exegesis are *androcentrism* and *patriarchy*. *Androcentrism* refers to the assumption that the experience of men is the norm for human experience; thus, androcentric language is noninclusive. Saint Paul, for example, invariably writes "dear brothers." *Patriarchy* refers to the philosophical idea that some men have a right to rule over the rest of men in society and, most particularly, over all women; in this context women have no choice but to be submissive.

Those who are attentive to the issues raised by the feminist critique will discover much evidence of androcentrism and patriarchy in the scriptures. This is not surprising, because the texts were written in times of overt male domination. Given the fact that God acts in concrete times and places and that the Bible reflects this, the biblical books reflect the biases of the cultures in which they were produced. Accordingly, one of the tasks of contemporary exegesis informed by feminist criticism is to retrieve memories of the experience of women suppressed by the patriarchal emphasis of the Bible. This allows women's experience to reshape our perceptions of God and the world.

There are three distinct "moments" in feminist biblical hermeneutics: first, the use of the "hermeneutics of suspicion," which asks, Whose interest is served in this text? The assumption here is that the biblical text is basically patriarchal and serving patriarchal interests. Second is the use of the "hermeneutics of remembrance," which asks, What is positive for women in this text? Third, having discovered something of merit behind the patriarchal language, there is the application of the "hermeneutics of celebration," which asks, What do we do with this text? Since it is the word of God, how do we celebrate the message about women rediscovered behind the text?[13]

The emergence of the mirror methods of biblical interpretation reinforces the validity of describing the Bible as a classic. The fact that methods of interpretation that have emerged only in the last generation are fruitfully applied to the Bible highlights the inexhaustible potential of the biblical texts to address human concerns. All these methods contribute to the interpretation of the Bible in the Christian community.

The reading of the Bible within the church will always remain a matter of faith, but it can be assisted by the insights of contemporary hermeneutics. Over and above what hermeneutics can supply, theologians will always need faith, imagination, and creativity—all of which are signs of the Spirit at work in the church. But hermeneutics remains vital, for it keeps theology, and the church as a whole, anchored in the reality of the biblical message.

QUESTIONS FOR REFLECTION

1. How is the Bible important in your life: personal, spiritual, and church-community?

2. How does a historical perspective help your reading of the Bible?

3. How may a contemporary hermeneutical approach to the biblical text deepen your understanding of God's Word?

4. How are biblical studies foundational to the study of theology?

SUGGESTIONS FOR FURTHER READING

- Boadt, Lawrence. *Reading the Old Testament: An Introduction.* New York: Paulist Press, 1984.

- Hayes, John H. and Carl R. Holladay. *Biblical Exegesis: A Beginner's Handbook,* rev. ed. London: SCM, 1988; Louisville: Westminster/John Knox Press, 1983.

- McKenzie, Steven L. and Stephen R. Haynes. *To Each Its Own Meaning: An Introduction to Biblical Criticisms and their Applications.* Louisville: Westminster/John Knox Press, 1993.

- Perkins, Pheme. *Reading the New Testament: An Introduction.* New York: Paulist Press, 1988.

NOTES

[1]*Dei Verbum,* Dogmatic Constitution on Divine Revelation, 11.

[2]*New Revised Standard Version* is the recommended text.

[3]Roger Haight, *Dynamics of Theology* (New York: Paulist Press, 1990), 120–21.

[4]The notion of the classic is developed most fully in the theology of David Tracy. A detailed and challenging study of Tracy's approach can be found in his book *The Analogical Imagination: Christian Theology and the Culture of Pluralism* (London: SCM, 1981; New York: Crossroad, 1995), 100–229.

[5]Haight, *Dynamics of Theology,* 97.

[6]Raymond Brown and Sandra Schneiders, "Hermeneutics," in *The New Jerome Biblical Commentary*, ed. R. E. Brown, J. A. Fitzmyer, and R. E. Murphy (London: Geoffrey Chapman, 1990; Englewood Cliffs, N.J.: Prentice Hall, 1990), 1146–65.

[7]Pontifical Biblical Commission, *The Interpretation of the Bible in the Church* (Homebush: St. Paul, 1993), 44.

[8]Raymond Collins, *Introduction to the New Testament* (London: SCM, 1983), 125.

[9]John Reumann, "After Historical Criticism, What? Trends in Biblical

Interpretation and Ecumenical, Interfaith Dialogues," *Journal of Ecumenical Studies* 29 (Winter 1992): 58.

[10]Elisabeth Schüssler-Fiorenza, *Revelation: Vision of a Just World* (Minneapolis: Fortress, 1991), 2.

[11]Schüssler-Fiorenza, *Revelation: Vision of a Just World,* 31.

[12]Pontifical Biblical Commission, *The Interpretation of the Bible in the Church,* 647–68.

[13]Cf. Carolyn Osiek, "The Feminist and the Bible: Hermeneutical Alternatives" in *Feminist Perspectives on Biblical Scholarship*, ed. Adela Yarbro Collins (Chico, CA: Scholars Press, 1985), 93–106.

Chapter Five

SEEKING UNDERSTANDING

> In this chapter we examine the kind of intellectual under-
> standing that theology yields. By examining the nature of
> theological explanations, with their strengths and limita-
> tions, we will illustrate the way philosophical thinking con-
> tributes to the practice of theology and to its dialogue with
> contemporary thought.

Theology seeks to give an intellectual account of the Christian
hope. For Catholic theology in particular, philosophical reflection has
been central to this endeavor. Catholic theology is both attentive to
humankind's perennial questioning and stimulated by contemporary
intellectual concerns. Although today only a minority of theology students undertake comprehensive studies in philosophy, all students of
Catholic theology are advised to acquire some grasp of the key philosophical distinctions and methods of reasoning and of the philosophical
themes on which theology continues to draw. These themes have
emerged over the centuries as thoughtful men and women have sought
to understand themselves and the world in which they live. Philosophy
is the disciplined study of such understanding as has been attained,
only to be further questioned, and at times dramatically overturned, by
new currents of thought.

This chapter has two parts. In the first part we will consider the
role of philosophy in the conversation between Christian belief and contemporary theories about the origins of the universe. In so doing, we will
be led to recall how Christian theology first emerged in dialogue with

ancient Greek science and philosophy, and to reflect both on the relationship between faith and human reasoning and on the limits of theological explanations. In the second part of this chapter we will situate theology in relation to the other forms of Christian speech. We will highlight the role of philosophy in the articulation of the central Christian mysteries of incarnation and eucharist, and we will conclude by affirming the possibilities for pluralism in theology.

Part One: The Quest for Coherence in Belief

Coherence Between Faith and Science

As we saw in chapter 2, human beings have always wondered about the origins of the universe and about their place in it. Such wonder is but one form of that restlessness of heart that is stilled only by the act of faith and self-surrender by which, as we saw in chapter 3, the human being comes into relationship with the mystery of God revealed in Jesus Christ. In the light of faith, Christians see the universe as created and sustained by God and as the prelude to, and the arena for, God's self-communication in word and grace. But how is God's creative act to be understood? The opening verses of the book of Genesis describe this act as one of bringing order to preexisting chaos:

> *In the beginning when God created the heavens and the earth, the earth was a formless void and darkness covered the face of the deep, while a wind from God swept over the face of the waters. (Gen 1:1–2)*

God's creation of a world in which all is good is a biblical word to which Christians must always be attentive even though, as chapter 4 reminded us, this "truth for salvation" is clothed in the author's human words and mode of expression, in this case the language and imagery of mythical divine intervention. The subsequent language of the Nicene Creed, while more prosaic, is more precise than the biblical witness: God is "creator of heaven and earth, of all things, seen and unseen." But if God is the creator of *all* things, then nothing whatsoever—not even a "formless void"—preceded God's creative act. God's creative act is entirely fresh and gratuitous; it is a creation "out of nothing."

Both the biblical and the credal statement of God's creative act stand in obvious tension with the statements of contemporary scientists like Stephen Hawking and Paul Davies, whose popular expositions of a new cosmology are international best-sellers. These authors speak of developing a Grand Unified Theory, a mathematical theory that provides an explanation of the universe as self-originating and self-sustaining. It is not yet clear whether such a theory will be developed, but if it were, what would then become of belief in God as "creator of all things seen and unseen"? Can this central profession of faith survive in a scientific age? Can a religious understanding of creation be squared with a scientific account of the beginning of the universe? The conversation between science and Christian faith opens with the recognition of these questions.

Theology is "faith seeking understanding," and theological understanding requires coherence of beliefs in two ways: first, coherence between religious beliefs and pertinent nonreligious beliefs and belief systems; and second, coherence between beliefs within a religious belief system. The new cosmology raises the need for the first kind of coherence, that between religious beliefs and well-founded scientific beliefs. As we will see shortly, the second kind of coherence requires a clarification of the presuppositions and implications of one religious belief in relation to other religious beliefs.

In the Catholic tradition, the quest for coherence between religious beliefs and beliefs deriving from science, human learning, and culture is essential to a living Christian faith. It is not an idle pastime for the curious, nor the special prerogative of defensive apologists. Faith convictions may not be insulated from one's other convictions, from "our best estimate of what we believe to be true of the events of history and the working of nature and the human mind."[1] Because the object of faith is the reality of God and the reality of God at work in Jesus the Christ, Christian convictions cannot be protected from the questions raised by our most reliable beliefs about reality in all its forms. Indeed, the convictions of faith are deepened and refined as they are brought into conversation with our other convictions.

It follows that every form of human inquiry that provides some understanding of reality is relevant to the believer's understanding of God. Accordingly, Christian theology needs to relate beliefs about God's creative action with whatever truth science reveals about the origins of the universe; to relate beliefs about sin and conversion with what psychology reveals about guilt, narcissism, and the development of the human personality; to relate beliefs about the inspired truth of the Bible with what literary and historical studies reveal about the way a text was formed and edited; to relate beliefs about the uniqueness of the person and "the resurrection of the body" with our best insights into human nature and identity; and so on.

But if Christian understanding is to include what might be termed "reflective coherence" between different kinds of beliefs, the following question must be addressed: In what terms are Christians to understand their faith convictions, to explain them to themselves and to others, and to square them with, or refine them in the light of, their nonreligious beliefs? In what terms, for example, is the religious belief in God as creator to be understood, and how does a belief in these terms relate to cosmologists' claims, in their terms of mathematical physics, about the universe as self-sustaining and emerging "out of nothing"?

In raising this question we are inevitably led to reflect on the contrasting ways in which science and faith view the universe. The success of modern science—that is, since the seventeenth century—has gone hand in hand with the rejection of the old teleological outlook (*telos* in Greek, meaning "end" or "goal") first articulated by the ancient Greek philosophers. This teleological outlook was implicitly theological, for it portrayed the beings that make up the universe as "naturally" developing toward their proper fulfillment under the guidance of an inner dynamism deriving from God as the supreme principle of being and goodness. Different thinkers understood this God in different ways, but the teleological presupposition itself was never doubted until modern times.

The particular teleological outlook criticized by modern scientists was epitomized by Aristotle's notion of "substantial form." For Aristotle, the prime metaphysical entities in the universe were individual "substances," for example, particular plants and animals, each with an "essential form," which makes it *what* it is as a certain *kind* of plant or animal. Form is an intrinsic and dynamic principle, which directs individual things toward their proper realization as good specimens of their kind. In the Aristotelian account, the "matter" of each thing individuated it as a particular example of the kind of thing it was—in virtue of the "form" it shared with others of its kind. For example, two or more statues may have the same design or form; what makes them distinct are the different lumps of bronze matter from which the sculptor has shaped them.

Medieval Christian theologians used this way of thinking about substances, with their form and matter, to reflect on the special place of human beings in the universe. Though distinct as individuals, all humans share the human form (or soul), by which they alone in creation are rational beings, ordered toward their proper fulfillment in knowing and loving the true and the good. Paradoxically, however, a rational being cannot be satisfied by any finite good or by any particular truth. Human nature is "open to the infinite." Thomas Aquinas concluded that the human predicament is precisely that, while human beings have a natural desire for the infinite good that alone would fulfill them—that is, God—they cannot obtain this fulfillment of themselves. The actual human *telos* revealed by Christianity—union with God—is, as we saw in chapter 3, a supernatural grace to be accepted through a free response to its offer.

Modern science breaks with this teleological outlook, and so too with its perspective on human fulfillment, in both its natural and supernatural aspects. Science now looks, not to the "natural" unfolding of a thing's essence, but to patterns of regularity and interaction that can be measured mathematically. Whereas the medieval scientist simply had to watch nature unfold, to watch a rose plant grow into a fine specimen of its kind, the modern scientist intervenes in nature to experiment, to alter natural conditions, to manipulate, and to measure the resulting "laws" of interaction between its smallest components. So although human beings are themselves part of nature, they are also its observers. Nature "is taken as that which is to be mastered and transformed by man....[Nature is] defined in function of technology and the human projects technology serves."[2] Nature has become a vast machine to be understood, not in terms of medium-sized entities, like plants, animals, and human beings (Aristotle's "primary substances"), but in terms of smaller and smaller entities, and ultimately in terms of the mathematical equations of quantum physics. Contemporary cosmology is one of the more remarkable achievements of the modern scientific enterprise. It portrays

> the universe of space-time and matter [as] internally consistent and self-contained. Its existence does not require anything outside of it; specifically, no prime mover is needed....Given the laws of physics, the universe can, so to speak, take care of itself, including its own creation.[3]

How might Christian understanding respond to the challenges raised by this account of the nature and origin of the universe? Our purpose here is not to propose a comprehensive theology of creation in the light of modern science, but simply to illustrate the way in which the quest for coherent understanding might begin. In the Catholic tradition, philosophy has always been central to such a quest. A central concern of philosophy in all periods has been to elucidate the nature of causality. So in order to relate the claims of faith and science, we may begin by noting the different ways in which each understands causation.

The scientist is concerned with the spatio-temporal causation of an effect by its antecedent cause (E because C) in accord with statistical laws, and this approach to causation can even be applied to what accounts for the initial event or "Big Bang" from which the universe developed. The theologian, by contrast, is concerned with the causation of *being*, whereby whatever actually exists in the spatio-temporal universe completely and continuously depends on God's causing it to be.[4] Given this distinction, it can be argued that God creates and sustains the universe of beings in the sense that God brings it about that there is a universe at all, albeit a universe governed by the statistical laws correlating cause and effect that scientists identify. Even if from the perspective of mathematical physics the law-like unfolding of universe is "self-sustaining," the theologian will suggest that from the perspective of why there is a universe at all, the universe cannot be self-sustaining, but must rather be understood as *caused to be* by God. God sustains the universe in existence with its combination of mathematical necessity, probability, chaos, and fruitful opportunity that science discerns and "explains."

In this way, the theologian may draw upon a philosophical clarification of the different kinds of causation in order to show how God's way of bringing about (that is, causing) a mathematically ordered and internally self-sustaining universe may be understood as distinct from, and yet presupposed by, the kind of bringing about that physicists are concerned with. In this way a philosophical mode of understanding assists fruitful dialogue between theology and science.

Moreover, there are good reasons to believe that modern science is now more open to dialogue with theological understanding than it has been in the past. First, the notion of a "holistic cause" (analogous to Aristotle's "form") is reemerging in many areas of modern science, especially in quantum mechanics and biology. A holistic cause is an organizing cause that makes a whole something more than the sum of its parts, a whole that manifests "a unity of operation and characteristics."[5] Second, the concept of God has been introduced into these discussions by some of the cosmologists themselves, thereby highlighting the philosophical claims that underlie their theories and that invite theological reflection. As Paul Davies acknowledges, for the modern cosmologist the "bedrock of reality" lies in mathematics:

> *The idea of transcendent laws of physics is the modern counterpart of Plato's realm of perfect Forms which acted as blueprints for the construction of the fleeting shadow-world of our perceptions.*[6]

At this point the theologian will want to note that these ultimate mathematical laws are far from self-explanatory. Why just these laws and not others? Don't these laws merely describe the universe as a self-sustaining space-time/energy-matter bounded whole, rather than account for why it exists at all? Doesn't a factor such as the universe's particular speed of expansion exemplify the fine-tuning essential to its existence and so add further mystery to the question of why such a universe exists?

The dialogue between theology and modern cosmology clearly raises many of the traditional philosophical questions long addressed by Christian theology. In particular, it raises the question of the nature and existence of God as the necessary cause of all that exists contingently, the created universe and all it comprises. Moreover, the theologian does not enter this dialogue fearing that science will make God redundant. Although Thomas Aquinas's understanding of physics is now outdated, his distinction between "primary" and "secondary" causation is not. For Thomas, God's causal role should be "scientifically redundant": it should not appear as a measurable factor in the scientific account, for the universe unfolds according to its own "secondary causes," whereas God is the transcendent "primary cause" sustaining the universe in being. For this reason Thomas would not expect a scientific account of how the universe unfolds to invoke a divine action either to initiate the process or to keep it going.

Faith and the Limits of Reason

In the case of contemporary cosmology, we have suggested that philosophical distinctions may help us to see how theological and nontheological beliefs can be coherent. Before going any further, we wish to caution the student about the extent to which theological explanations can be developed. To stay with our current example, even supposing an account of divine creation and causality were to be developed and found philosophically convincing, the question should arise as to the extent to which such an account would offer an explanation of God's creative action. If philosophy provides theology with conceptual tools of explanation, does it not follow that to the extent that we succeed in explaining God's creative causality, our original faith profession will have been reduced to a belief in a philosophical explanation that does not itself require faith? Given such an explanation, the object of faith would no longer be the revealed mystery of God as creator, but rather a certain theory of causation.

Moreover, it would seem that any and every theological explanation is doomed to be reductionist in that it replaces a revealed truth that expresses an aspect of the divine mystery (for example, of God as creator) with a humanly accessible truth or explanation (for example, a theory of divine causality). This reductionist tendency will apply as much to nonphilosophical explanations as to philosophical explanations, since the uniqueness and transcendent reality of the mysteries of faith imply that the truths of faith cannot, in principle, be explained in any other terms. It is the understandable fear of this reductionism that ultimately lies behind fundamentalism in all its forms. Fundamentalism seeks to isolate religious claims, whether as private experiences or as verbal formulations (in the Bible or in the church's teaching), from any interaction with nonreligious claims.

There can be little doubt that at times theology has tended toward a rationalistic, philosophical reduction of faith, but it need not do so. The contribution of philosophical reflection to theological inquiry is neither that of providing a rational explanation that is valid quite independently of faith and thereby reductive of God and God's creative action, nor is it that of taking us just so far toward an understanding of God and the universe, with a "leap of faith" taking us the rest of the way to full understanding.

These two mistaken views of the role of theological explanations in general, and of philosophical explanations in particular, both portray reason and faith as competitors in the same domain: philosophical reason overseeing those truths we can rationally establish, faith toying with other (purported) truths that we cannot rationally establish. It has been pointed out that the assumption that reason and faith are in competition is shared both by secular thinkers who conclude that faith is an irrational leap, a pale substitute for the evidence reason demands, and by those Christian thinkers who conclude that faith fills "the gap between a warranted case for theism and an unwarranted case for Christianity."[7] In the case of Christianity, this latter view is unsatisfactory because it implies that faith simply fills in the "gaps" that remain in our human, rational explanations: whatever we cannot account for is believed to be accounted for by God, but only until such time as we can explain it for ourselves. But as the gaps become fewer and smaller, the need for faith diminishes and God becomes more and more irrelevant.

Furthermore, the same assumption seems to be at work in some interpretations of the Catholic Church's teaching that human beings can know God by the light of natural reason. From this teaching of the First Vatican Council (1869–70), it is commonly thought to follow first, that by philosophical reasoning alone one can prove the existence of God, and second, that with this proof achieved, faith is (merely) the additional step we take, with God's grace, to enter into a life-giving relationship with the God whose existence we have already demonstrated for ourselves. On this interpretation, the act of faith builds on and perfects a prior act of reason complete in itself; and likewise theology builds on and perfects philosophy.[8]

By contrast, the conception of the relationship between reason and faith in this book—a conception now widely held by Catholic theologians—is that faith is always an act of the whole person that goes beyond, even though it also includes, the exercise of human reasoning. Even if "the reality of God is accessible to rational inquiry" apart from faith,[9] it is only within the context of faith that such rational inquiry attains the living and saving God. As we saw in chapter 3, the act of faith is, from its outset to its completion, empowered by grace: it begins as an initial or implicit response and grows to become a fully conscious and articulated response to the self-communication of God. Faith must be understood in this way because faith "grounded on anything other than itself is thereby reduced to something less than faith, that is, to a form of reason."[10]

Faith is a response to the reality of God's self-communication, but God's self-communication does not fall within the domain of empirical or rational knowledge. Faith is not a leap within the order of the intellect to a new item of knowledge for which evidence is lacking. Rather, faith presupposes "a leap *from* the order of the intellect to the order of the heart,"[11] that is, from what would be merely an act of knowing to what has become a personal act of self-commitment. To say that faith is from the heart is to imply that for the believer rational inquiry into God always, and already, depends on a response of the whole person to the mystery of God. For this reason, there is not normally a time prior to faith during which a person rationally ponders the existence of God; and likewise, when Christians think philosophically, they do not retreat from the order of faith, they do not bracket their beliefs, pretending not to believe in God, in order to question God's existence.

Nonetheless, faith from the heart is not irrational or unreasonable, and the reality of God experienced in faith is not immune to rational inquiry. On the contrary, for the believer philosophical inquiry bears upon the assumptions and implications of his or her experience of faith and relationship with God in Christ, and accordingly "whatever philosophical knowledge we have of God emerges…as the intellectual dimension of faith."[12] It follows that although rational inquiry about God has its integrity apart from faith, for the theologian doing theology, philosophical reflection is chiefly deployed *within* the exploration of faith.

Clearly, the most fundamental assumption of faith is that there really is a God with whom the believer is in relationship; moreover, the believer is entitled to test this assumption through rational inquiry. The result of this inquiry is what the First Vatican Council affirmed as "the knowledge of God by the light of human reason," even though this knowledge is in fact only attained and exercised within the obedience and self-commitment of faith. Hence, faith is not an addition that builds on philosophical reasoning complete in itself; faith is not like a second story added on to what had been a single-story house. The "house" of faith is built on faith from the outset; sound philosophical reasoning about goodness and being, about causation and becoming, leading to a natural knowledge of God, is more like its infrastructure or frame:

> The philosophical enquiry into the grounds for belief in God is neither an examination of the reasons which led the believer into commitment, nor is it an independent investigation unrelated to those reasons. It is an examination of an assumption which, in accepting those reasons, the believer makes.…[The philosopher]

*is examining or articulating the assumptions of the believing
mind.*[13]

It follows that we must distinguish using philosophy in theology
from doing philosophy itself. A Christian who does philosophy may
not invoke theology or religious belief in authoritative support of his or
her conclusions. In doing philosophy, one is judged by the standards of
human reasoning alone. The quality of one's philosophy will depend on
the soundness of its starting points and initial data, on the depth of its
insights, and on the validity of its arguments. The "Christian philosophy after the mind of St. Thomas Aquinas" recommended by Pope Leo
XIII in his encyclical *Aeterni Patris* (1879) was to be a genuine philosophy, not a theologically manipulated philosophy. The hallmark of this
philosophy is that it reflects not merely on human ideas or concepts or
language, but on the material realities of which the universe is comprised. *Metaphysics* is that branch of philosophy that seeks to understand the nature of reality, and in particular the nature of those concrete
realities or beings, including persons, which the human mind encounters as independent from itself. It is the "realism" of this kind of philosophy, Leo XIII believed, that is best able to illuminate the reality of the
universe and of God affirmed in faith.[14]

We will comment later on the prospects for this "realist" philosophy. Our immediate purpose is to examine the philosophical orientation
of Catholic theology in the elucidation of faith. It will be helpful at this
point to recall how Western philosophical and theological inquiries first
emerged in the ancient Greek world, centuries before the Christian
movement began.

The Emergence of Christian Theology

Theology is literally "discourse about god," but not all discourse
about God is theology in the sense of systematic, rationally persuasive
discourse. To appreciate the distinctiveness of rational discourse, it is
necessary to appreciate the decisive intellectual steps taken by the first
Greek philosophers five centuries before Jesus of Nazareth was born.
These pre-Socratic thinkers pioneered rational thought by replacing
"unargued fables" with "argued theory."[15] Their inquiry was rational
because it depended on generalization and measurement and, above
all, on the search for universal law behind the apparent arbitrariness of

happenstance. They sought to uncover the underlying order of the cosmos. They were the first cosmologists as well as the first theologians, because they developed a concept of god as the necessary explanatory principle of the universe. That is to say, they replaced mythical stories about gods (divine beings) who intervened in the world in arbitrary ways, with a rationally controlled concept of god as both unique and transcendent, and not as one item among the many in the cosmos.

The emergence of this concept of a god or ultimate principle was decisive for Western thought. It now "became possible to *think* of god, and at the same time difficult if not impossible not to think of god."[16] That is, it became virtually impossible not to think of the universe as ordered and intelligible in virtue of some ultimate explanatory principle or principles. These early inquiries were not yet differentiated into what later became philosophy, theology, and cosmology: they were a single form of inquiry into the order and intelligibility of the universe. Irrespective of whether their inquiries led individual thinkers to agnosticism (for example, Democritus) or to monotheism (for example, Xenophanes), what was crucial was the pursuit of rational inquiry in the conviction that order and explanation could be found.

It may be difficult for us, more than two thousand years later, to realize that rational argument had to be discovered. Yet the truth is that Aristotle single-handedly founded the science of logic, the study of valid inference, when he identified that distinctive pattern of reasoning in which "some things being given, something else *follows of necessity*" (for example: If every A is a B, and every B is a C, then *it follows of necessity* that every A is a C). The discovery of this form of necessity, called *syllogism,* and its systematic articulation in Aristotle's laws of the logical inference, dominated all of "science" (in Latin, *scientia* means "knowledge") for the next two thousand years.

From the thirteenth century to the middle of the twentieth century, Catholic theology was shaped by this Aristotelian conception of science as a form of inquiry in which, on the basis of "first principles," one sought to establish new and certain knowledge using the valid forms of the syllogism Aristotle had discovered. Armed with the syllogism as a mechanism for generating new conclusions from preexisting truths, the critical task for theology, as for every *scientia,* was to defend its starting points as "given," as obviously true with respect to their subject matter, and then to deduce what followed of necessity from these "first principles": to deduce, for example, what follows about the nature and action of God.

On this account, the truths of theology were related to the truths of other forms of inquiry by virtue of the relationships between the various *scientiae,* and these relationships depended on the relative superiority or inferiority of a *scientia*'s explanatory power. For example, physics (the science of local movement) was inferior to mathematics (the science of number), because mathematics was needed to describe movement. Metaphysics (the science of being) was the highest philosophical science, because the first principles of being were presupposed by all other sciences.[17] Theology, however, was superior to all the philosophical sciences, because its first principles were the ultimate truths about reality held in the mind of God. Since each *scientia* could take as its starting point truths established by an inferior *scientia,* theology could also invoke among its starting points the "inferior" truths of philosophy.

Christian theology thus came to see itself as the "Queen of the Sciences," with philosophy as its "handmaid." In keeping with the nature of an Aristotelian *scientia,* theology's mode of reasoning was essentially deductive. However, the accession of theology to the position of Queen of the Sciences was not uncontested, and her reign was short-lived. This is not surprising if we reflect on why the intellectual enterprise of Christian theology had been inherently problematic from the outset, indeed almost a contradiction in terms.[18]

Coherence Between Religious Beliefs: The Development of Christology

Greek theology sought an explanation of the impersonal underlying order of the cosmos. Aristotle's god was a cosmic Unmoved Mover, while Plato's (c. 428–347 B.C.E.) ultimate principle of explanation was the Form of the Good, the concrete Ideal of Goodness itself, from which Plotinus (204/5–270 C.E.) would later posit the emanation of all other things as lesser perfections. Christian theology, by contrast, had to conceive of a personal God acting in history without falling back into the old mythical way of thinking; it had to conceive of God as creator of the universe without reducing God to a deterministic, cosmological principle; and finally, it had to conceive of God in Christ as eschatological savior, acting definitively in a way universally relevant to humankind, not as the god of a particular people or place.[19] Christians had to be able to think of God in these new ways in order both to make sense of, and to be faithful to, their faith experience of Jesus.

In their earliest profession of faith, it was enough for Christians to exclaim: "Jesus is Lord." But they were soon led to question the coherence of this claim with their preexisting religious beliefs. Since "Lord" was the title for Yahweh, God of Israel, to say Jesus is Lord is to proclaim his equality with God or, in more abstract terms, to proclaim "the divinity" of Jesus. But what exactly does this mean? It surely doesn't mean that Jesus is identical with Yahweh, or that Yahweh the one God has become the human being Jesus of Nazareth. Furthermore, the New Testament contains a number of statements in which Christians spoke of Jesus becoming Lord after his resurrection. Does this mean he was not always equal to God? How, indeed, could anyone, at any time, become God?

In response to questions like these, Christians developed a new paradigm and locus of theological inquiry, a newly structured way of thinking, in terms of which their fundamental convictions could be articulated. This paradigm was focused on *Christology,* and the intellectual coherence of the Christian belief system was articulated in the doctrines of the incarnation and the Trinity hammered out during the first three centuries of the Christian era, culminating in the great credal formulations of the councils of Nicea (325 C.E.) and Chalcedon (451 C.E.).

The solemn formulae of these early councils are replete with philosophical terms like *person, form, nature, substance,* and *being,* which were current at the time. These terms were drawn upon as the best available for safeguarding what Christians should and should not say when professing their faith. To say that Jesus is "of one substance (or being)" with God the Father is to say, not that Jesus is identical with God the Father, but that he is equal to the Father in every way (other than the way in which he is related to the Father as Son). It will be apparent that neither this credal formulation, nor our one-sentence restatement of it, explains the incarnation or what it is for Jesus of Nazareth to be the Son of God. Nonetheless, it will also be apparent that, insofar as Christians must profess their faith, and given the terms then available to them in which to profess it, this was surely the right formulation to adopt. For Christians to have said of Jesus that he was anything less than "of one substance" with God the Father would be for them to have denied their experience of him as risen *Lord*, as God among them.

But why should it be thought that such philosophical terms are the most suitable ones in which to formally profess the faith? An answer to this question lies in a consideration of the goals of metaphysics as Aristotle described them. Aristotle's so-called metaphysical writings were catalogued after (*meta* in Greek) his writings on physics, the study of nature (*phusis* in Greek). This cataloguing decision provides a useful clue to what metaphysics aspires to be. Whereas the physicist studies what happens in nature as the spatio-temporal arena of causation and change, growth and decay, the "meta-physicist" studies nature itself, or "being *qua* being" (being *inasmuch as it is* being). This last phrase almost defies translation. *Being* designates all that is, reality in all its forms; so metaphysics inquires into the reality of the real, or the nature of nature, or the essence and substance of whatever exists. The tautological force of these phrases points to the way metaphysical inquiry aims to be the most fundamental of all philosophical inquiries, to provide the most comprehensive understanding of reality simply as reality. When someone claims that reality is ultimately just matter, or process, or ideas, or atoms in the void, and so on, he or she is making a typically metaphysical claim.

It is because philosophy, and metaphysics in particular, seeks to understand the ultimate nature of reality that it is such a close ally of theology, for the faith that theology seeks to articulate is a response of the whole person to what is taken to be most ultimately real. Yet once again a caution must be issued: all human understanding, and so all philosophical understanding, relies on distinctions that can properly be made only within the cosmos, between created entities. The distinction between God and creation as a whole, however, is a distinction between Uncreated and created.

Human beings have no independent vantage point from which to describe the relationship and distinction between Uncreated and created. Moreover, according to the Christian doctrine of creation, not only did God not need to create a universe, but furthermore, the created universe adds nothing to the perfection that exists in God. The universe as a whole need not have existed, and if it had not existed there would be no less goodness or being whatsoever. It follows that the distinction between God and the universe is not a distinction between two realities, both of which exist independently apart from the way they are related to each other. God is other than the universe, but God's identity does not depend on God being other than anything at all. In the terms of Thomas Aquinas's metaphysics, the relationship between the universe and God is "real" on the part of the universe (namely, a relationship of real dependence), but "not real" on the part of God. The point of Aquinas's teaching here is that

> *in the Christian distinction God is understood as "being" God entirely apart from any relation of otherness to the world or to the whole. God could and would be God even if there were no world. Thus the Christian distinction is appreciated as a distinction that did not have to be, even though it in fact is. The most fundamental thing we come to in Christianity, the distinction between the world and God, is appreciated as not being the most fundamental thing after all, because one of the terms of the distinction, God, is more fundamental than the distinction itself.*[20]

In these considerations we find the key to why any explanation of God's creative action will be so limited. The distinction between God and the universe is unique. We can only begin to think about this distinction in terms available to us, namely, in terms of distinctions between the sorts of beings we encounter within the universe as a whole. But having been led to affirm the distinction between God and the universe as a whole, and to realize why this is a unique distinction, we then recognize that our concepts and distinctions are quite inadequate for comprehending this distinction between God and the whole. We find here a pattern that will recur in the discussions to come: philosophy and theology help us to begin thinking about the mysteries of faith. They thus provide a "horizon of intelligibility," which at the same time reveals how inadequate our thinking along those lines must be, and why—for the mystery of faith lies beyond any and every horizon of human understanding.

Part Two: Theology as a Mode of Christian Speech

The Three Modes of Christian Speech

From its beginning, Christianity has required not merely an interior attitude or disposition (faith), but also a life marked by appropriate speech and action. Like Judaism and Islam, Christianity involves both *orthodoxy* (right words) and *orthopraxis* (right actions), for salvation depends on both a "belief from the heart" and a "confession with the lips" (cf. Rom 10:10). In chapters 1 and 3, we have seen how theology considers the right ordering of Christian speech about the mystery of God's self-communication, and in the next chapter we will see how Christian ethics (or moral theology) brings the light of faith to bear on the right ordering of human living. In this chapter we have examined the demand for coherence both between religious and nonreligious beliefs and between different religious beliefs. We now wish to highlight the distinctive character of theological discourse within the life of the church, to see how it shapes the articulation of doctrine, and to recognize how and why it opens the way to further doctrinal development.

Three distinct contexts for Christian speech may be distinguished: prayer and worship, the formulation of doctrine, and the work of theology. *Prayer and worship* provide the primary context for Christian speech. To be a Christian is to be in relationship to God through Christ in the Holy Spirit and within a communion of discipleship. A Christian's first mode of speech, therefore, is the language of personal address, the language of invocation; this is not talk *about* God, but address *to* (and from) God and one another in petition and thanksgiving, praise and lamentation, repentance and forgiveness, command and obedience, and blessing and curse. This language of prayer is the primary mode of speech that shapes, and is shaped by, experience and action. Included in this mode is the profession of one's faith in the context of prayer and worship. As noted already, we may consider the most fundamental confession of faith to be the simple but original proclamation that Jesus is Lord.

The chief function of this invocatory speech is to exercise one's faith. Thus, Augustine wrote of the disciple "exercising" his or her desire for God in prayer. A characteristic feature of this mode of speech is the use of image and metaphor, as the disciple spontaneously and instinctively reaches for the words and images that fit his or her experience. Christians do not possess a special language with special words and meanings suited just for faith and theology; words do not change their meaning when used in religious contexts. Ordinary human language in all its variety is used in distinctive ways—ways that people find apt for their own experiences in faith.

The twentieth century's seminal philosopher of language, Ludwig Wittgenstein, remarked that people find themselves in relationship to one another when they are in instinctive agreement about what it is apt to say in particular circumstances. In the first instance, there are no independent, rational, standards for what metaphors are apt to the Christian experience. Whatever Christians find apt—for example, the language of the Psalms and such traditional metaphors for God as shepherd, fortress, and rock— is apt. What is apt for some—for example, Bernard of Clairvaux's (1090–1153) image of the Holy Spirit as "the Kiss of God," the kiss between Father and Son—may not be apt for all. Metaphor forms community, and the language of prayer is fundamentally communitarian, a shared language reflecting a shared sensibility. The locus of this primary mode of speech is thus the experience of discipleship; this is the speech of all Christ's faithful people.

Metaphors suggest thoughts and lines of explanation that are tested and refined through the *formulation of doctrine,* the second mode of Christian speech. The creeds are essentially elaborations of the fundamental claim that Jesus is Lord, that spontaneous exclamation of those who encountered the risen Christ but who little grasped the import of their instinctive transference of God's title to the man Jesus of Nazareth. The elaboration of this confession in the teaching of the church, in the doctrines of faith, involves a more formalized mode of speech whose chief function is to distinguish appropriate from inappropriate ways of addressing God, one another, and the world.

Doctrines and creeds are, in effect, "identity-sustaining rules" enabling the church's primary discourse in prayer.[21] By this regulation, the identity of the church is both formed and sustained as a community faithful to the word it has received and is charged to hand on. The chief function of doctrinal statement, therefore, is regulative; and, as we will see, doctrinal formulations more often regulate by determining what Christians may *not* say, than by insisting on what they *must* say. Though much doctrinal formulation is condemnatory, and the language of condemnation is jarring, it is important to note that this negative, regulative force is restricted to ruling out only what is meant by that precise opinion or form of speech that it identifies. A condemnation that prohibits a Christian from saying "Jesus is not of one being with the Father" (or its equivalent), leaves ample room for other affirmations about Jesus, both in prayer and in theology.

The locus of doctrinal speech is the church, which teaches both informally in catechesis by parents and teachers, and formally in the pronouncements of the church's teaching magisterium (when the pastors of the church "define" the faith). Definitions, however, should be considered less as explanations than as adjudications about what may and what may not be said in the primary mode, prayer or invocation, which always takes priority: "What you can say correctly about the God outside the invocative context [the primary context of address], can only be validated by what you can rightly say within it."[22]

Theological inquiry constitutes the third mode of Christian speech answerable to, yet distinct both from the original context of prayer and worship, and from the secondary context of doctrinal definition. The former awaits theological refinement, while the latter makes theological assumptions that await critical evaluation. Theology thus mediates between prayer and doctrine, and its characteristic features are conceptualization and systematic thought. Its chief function is to develop a reflective articulation of the faith confession in the light of its presuppositions and context of formulation and with a view to its contemporary implications.

The customary locus of theological speech is "the academy"; it is the speech of scholars and teachers and to a lesser extent of preachers. As we noted in chapter 1, theology should not be isolated from prayer and from critical engagement in witness and service. Indeed, the isolation of theology from spirituality and service is a phenomenon of recent centuries that many theologians are now seeking to redress. Liberation theologians in particular have shown how theology needs the stimulus of a faith-filled engagement with the gospel and work for justice, shaped by the perspective of the poor and marginalized.

The intellectual ancestry of this account of the three modes of Christian speech includes John Henry Newman's understanding of the three offices of Christ as *Priest, Prophet,* and *King* and their threefold interaction, as applied to the life of the church. In 1877 Newman republished his study of the Anglican Church as the *via media,* the middle way, between Protestantism and Catholicism. Writing as a Roman Catholic, Newman sought to place his earlier criticism of Catholicism in context and to correct those claims he now judged to be unfounded. He argued that there will always be much to criticize in the life of the church, because it is difficult for the church as a whole, as for the individual

Christian, to maintain a healthy balance between the different forces at work within it. Just as Christ is Priest, Prophet, and King, so the church is at once *priestly,* as a religious form of life; *prophetic,* with a "philosophy" of life; and *kingly,* that is, organized politically as a single community. Newman's concise formulation summarizes the concerns of the second part of this chapter:

> *Christianity...is at once a philosophy, a political power, and a*
> *religious rite: as a religion, it is Holy; as a philosophy, it is Apos-*
> *tolic; as a political power, it is imperial, that is, One and Catholic.*
> *As a religion, its special seat is pastor and flock; as a philosophy,*
> *the Schools; as a rule, the Papacy and its Curia.*[23]

Newman noted that each of these aspects of the church's identity has its own special focus, with its own "methodology," or guiding principle, and likewise its own besetting temptation:

> *Truth is the guiding principle of theology and theological*
> *inquiries; devotion and edification [is the guiding principle] of*
> *worship; and expedience [is the guiding principle] of government.*
> *The instrument of theology is reasoning; of worship, our emo-*
> *tional nature; of rule, command and coercion. Further, reasoning*
> *tends to rationalism, devotion to superstition and enthusiasm, and*
> *power to ambition and tyranny.*[24]

Newman emphasized that each of these aspects needs the corrective influence of the other two. For example, theology needs to be inspired by prayer and personal experience (to avoid rationalism) and also to be shaped by pastoral prudence (to avoid damage to the unity of the church). Newman saw that it was not the role of either doctrine or theology to restrict unnecessarily the disciple's freedom for prayer and action. Commenting on the First Vatican Council's definition of papal infallibility, Newman wrote in 1875 to the Duke of Norfolk:

> *The infallibility, whether of the Church or of the Pope, acts princi-*
> *pally or solely in two channels, in direct statements of truth, and in*
> *the condemnation of error. The former takes the shape of doctrinal*
> *definitions, the latter stigmatizes propositions as heretical, next to*
> *heresy, erroneous, and the like. In each case the Church...has*
> *made provision for weighing as lightly as possible on the faith and*
> *conscience of her children.*[25]

Definitions and condemnations should "weigh as lightly as possible" on the Christian's profession of faith in word and deed, permitting as much freedom in both speech and action as is compatible with defined truth. Newman continues:

> *As to the condemnation of propositions all [the Church] tells us is,*
> *that the thesis condemned when taken as a whole, or, again, when*
> *viewed in its context, is heretical, or blasphemous, or impious, or*
> *whatever....We have only to trust here so far as to allow ourselves*
> *to be warned against the thesis, or the work containing it. Theolo-*
> *gians employ themselves in determining what precisely it is that is*
> *condemned in that thesis or treatise; and doubtless in most cases*
> *they do so with success; but that determination is not* de fide; *all*
> *that is of faith [in the condemnation] is that there is in that thesis*
> *itself, which is noted, heresy or error...such that the censure is a*
> *peremptory command to theologians, preachers, students, and all*
> *others whom it concerns, to keep clear of it.*[26]

Finally, Newman noted that theology is "the fundamental and regulating principle of the whole Church system."[27] He did not mean that theologians should have the last word on matters of Christian faith and practice. He meant, rather, that ultimately faith and practice are answerable to revelation, to the truth of the divine mystery revealed; and it is this truth that, in the end, must govern both religious devotion and pastoral order. It is properly theology's task to seek to articulate and interpret this inexhaustible truth in every age.

Philosophy and the Understanding of Doctrine

In the light of the distinction between these three modes of speech, we can now highlight the distinctive role of philosophical understanding in the articulation of doctrine. While we will not be undertaking a similarly detailed study of the relationship between philosophy and the first mode of Christian speech, prayer and worship (to which we may add preaching and pastoral encouragement), it should be noted that some of the words that believers instinctively reach for in prayer and worship are philosophically charged. For example, in the prologue to John's Gospel the term *Logos* is used for the Son of God, for Jesus "the Word made flesh." But although *logos* was a technical term in Stoic philosophy, we need not suppose that the author of this Gospel was using it in a technical way.

To be sure, *logos* resonates with philosophical significance reaching back to the origins of Greek philosophy, where it signified not only 'word,' but also, as we saw in chapter 2, discourse and reason. The term *logos,* however, was also part of the vocabulary of the reasonably well-educated first-century person, much as *evolution, ideology,* and *authenticity* are today widely used by speakers who do not adhere to the philosophies of Spencer, Marx, or Heidegger, respectively. This same informal use of what in other contexts might be technical terms occurs in 2 Peter 1:4, where the author refers to Christians as "participants of the divine nature"; the theme of "participation" was central to Platonic and neo-Platonic thought.

It is with doctrinal formulations that the technicalities of philosophical discourse become relevant. There are two distinct issues here: the first concerns the diversity in the expression of doctrine mentioned in chapter 3; the second, the use of philosophy in the formulation of doctrinal statements. These two issues are linked because often theological interpretation will involve distinguishing a binding doctrinal content from its formulation in a particular terminology. This may be illustrated by considering the use of the term *transubstantiation* by the Council of Trent in its formulation of eucharistic doctrine. The council held that through consecration the "whole substance" of the bread is changed to become the body of Christ, and the "whole substance" of the wine is changed to become the blood of Christ. The council then added that this change is "suitably and properly called" transubstantiation.[28]

In reflecting on the significance of Trent's choice of words, we must distinguish between the dogmatic truth of faith and the theological and philosophical concepts used to express it. Trent was primarily concerned to affirm the eucharistic change as the basis for Christ's eucharistic presence. It expressed this truth in terms of "transubstantiation," that is, the change of the "whole substance" of the bread and wine. This concept does not explain the mystery of the Eucharist, which involves a unique change that could not be explained as an instance of some more general kind of change. As we said earlier, any purported explanation of this mystery could not but be reductionist. The object of a Catholic's eucharistic faith is the eucharistic identity of Christ, not an explanatory theory about a process called transubstantiation. It follows that, in principle, eucharistic faith might be articulated in terms other than the Aristotelian terms of "substance" and "transubstantiation." Indeed, the change of substance that occurs in the Eucharist is not one that could occur in Aristotle's system.

These points prompt the following questions: First, if the Aristotelian philosophy of substance cannot explain the eucharistic change, of what value is it to the formulation of doctrine? How can Trent say this change is "properly" called transubstantiation? Second, even if in principle eucharistic faith can be articulated in other, non-Aristotelian terms, how could we know that a proposed, novel articulation truly preserved the meaning of the doctrine? How could we determine what other terms "properly" apply to the eucharistic change?

With respect to the first question, we note that every formulation of doctrine must be undertaken in terms that provide what we have called a "horizon of intelligibility," a line of systematic thinking in terms of which various conceptual contrasts and comparisons can be made and various questions framed and answered. For the bishops at Trent, as for theologians during the preceding three centuries, Aristotle's philosophy of nature was thought to provide the most refined possibilities for thinking about change and identity, about what something "really is" and about how it is affected by the changes it undergoes.

Since Catholic eucharistic faith is centered on the identity and presence of Christ in the Eucharist, thinking about this presence inevitably raises questions as to what the eucharistic elements of bread and wine are before and after consecration and about what kind of change occurs through consecration. These are all substance questions, what-something-is questions. If one thinks in terms of substance, and if one wants to express one's eucharistic faith, one is led to say that after the consecration "the whole substance" of Christ is present, and that Christ is not just present "along with" the substance of bread and wine *(consubstantiation),* nor just present "in" the substance of bread and wine *(impanation).*

By thinking about substance in (admittedly, rather loose) Aristotelian terms, a number of contrasts emerge: substance present "in its own right," substance present "along with" another, substance present "in" another. But for Aristotle, substance—a something in its own right—cannot but be "in its own right," it cannot be *with* or *in* something else; for whatever exists "in something else" (for example, a shape) is an "accident," not a substance. Clearly Aristotle does not mean by substance what we commonly mean when talking of the *chemical* substance of some entity (for example, H_2O or iron oxide). Aristotle's conceptual framework simply provides a "horizon of intelligibility" within which one knows at least some of the things *not* to say about the Eucharist, and leaves in place the one thing that can and should be said: namely, that in the Eucharist there is a change of the "whole substance" of bread and wine.

To be able to believe in the eucharistic change, one must, to some extent however limited, be able to think about the eucharistic change. To think is to employ concepts, to make distinctions, and to draw comparisons. Of course, as Thomas Aquinas reminds us, the believer's act of faith terminates, not in a proposition believed, but in the reality it signifies. Faith reaches beyond the propositions used in its profession to attain the reality of God as First Truth. But for a proposition that one believes to have any meaning or signifying capacity, it must be thinkable to some extent. So although the doctrine of Trent does not provide an explanation of eucharistic change, it does make a rule for right speech about the eucharistic mystery, and it does shed some limited light on that mystery.

How then could we recognize other ways of speaking rightly about the eucharistic mystery, ways that do not involve thinking in Aristotelian terms? The need for other formulations seems obvious. Both philosophically and theologically the naturalistic categories of Aristotelian physics and substance metaphysics fail to do justice to so many aspects of the eucharistic mystery. For example, they do not take into account either our more accurate understanding of the scriptural texts describing the institution of the Eucharist and its background in Jewish beliefs about sacred meals, the power of blessing, and presence-in-mystery; or our appreciation of the relationship between the incarnation and the sacraments as personal and symbolic modes of God's self-communication. For these reasons, the this-worldly language of "substances" and "natural changes" impoverishes the personal and transcendent dimensions of the eucharistic mystery.[29]

The difficulty in determining whether a new formulation is faithful to the truth of a doctrine arises because, although every doctrine transcends its manner of formulation, we have no access to the binding content of a doctrine apart from its formulation in some philosophical framework or other. It follows that although, on the one hand, no dogmatic formulation, like no biblical formulation, may ever be cast aside as outdated and irrelevant, on the other hand, there is no theology-free or concept-free formulation of doctrine, immune from refinement and development.

Furthermore, criteria for determining new orthodox formulations cannot be proposed in advance. It is normally only *after* the event that developments in doctrine and formulation are recognized and accepted. The bishops at Trent could not, for the most part, think in anything other than "substance" terms. To the extent that we can think about reality, personal reality in particular, in other than substance terms, to that extent we can begin to envisage new formulations of doctrine precisely because we are able to distinguish content from formulation in a way not previously possible. Still, because we have no access to the content of doctrine apart from its various formulations, including its biblical, and often metaphorical, formulations, we do not attempt to isolate "content" from "formulation" until pressed to do so.

C. S. Lewis made this point in his characteristic fashion when he asked, "Did the early Christians believe that God really has a material palace in the sky and that he received his Son in a decorated state chair placed a little to the right of his own—or did they not?" The alternatives, he said, were not present to their minds. "The Church knew the answer (that God has no body and therefore, couldn't sit in a chair) as soon as it knew the question." As Lewis remarks, it is only when the "nut" of doctrine is cracked that "shell" and "kernel" are recognized, and the Christian knows which part to throw away. "Till then he holds on to the nut: not because he is a fool, but because he isn't."[30]

Ultimately it is for the church as a whole to recognize its faith in new formulations that could not previously have been imagined. The theme of "recognition" has become central to recent ecumenical endeavors as the different churches and traditions examine their different ways of understanding their faith confessions.[31] The formal and decisive recognition of doctrine and formulation is the responsibility of the church's teaching authority. For example, the church has always rejected "merely symbolic" understandings of the Eucharist as unfaithful to the realism of Catholic belief. Recent alternatives to transubstantiation suggesting that the eucharistic change consists in a change in the *meaning* of bread and wine *(transignification)* or a change in the *purpose* of the bread and wine *(transfinalization)* have thus been rejected.

Given the rejection of these formulations, it is important to recall New-man's observation that condemnations are to be understood in the most restrictive way compatible with the safeguarding of doctrinal truth. Newman wrote of "a legitimate minimizing" with respect to the precise point or opinion being rejected.[32] The rejection of some ways of speaking of a change in the meaning of the eucharistic elements does not amount to the wholesale rejection of all eucharistic theologies in which meaning is a central theme. One would need to examine closely the precise details of each theological proposal, along with its philosophical presuppositions, in order to determine whether it preserves the traditional faith of the church as formulated in terms of transubstantiation.

In short, while every formulation of doctrine remains an irreplaceable witness to what the church found apt, or felt compelled, to say in a particular context in order to safeguard its faith, the continuing interpretation and development of doctrinal formulation are essential to the life of the church.

From Doctrine to Theology

The theological articulation of doctrine has already figured in our discussion of the formulation of eucharistic doctrine, for there is a continuity between the formulation and the elaboration of doctrine. A theology of transubstantiation, for example, would be an attempt to extend the brief doctrinal formulae of Trent into a coherent and systematic thinking through of the doctrine, deploying various Aristotelian concepts and principles in order to provide it with a "horizon of intelligibility." Every doctrinal formulation either brings with it an implicit theological articulation or anticipates its subsequent articulation. In this section, we will look more closely at this latter endeavor, not with respect to eucharistic faith, but to the ancient confession of faith in Jesus as Lord (Rom 10:9; Phil 2:11) discussed in the first half of this chapter. We will see how philosophical thinking contributed to the transition from the monotheism of Israel to the coherent trinitarian faith of the church.

The traditional formulation that Jesus Christ is "one person with two natures" was until recently a commonplace of Catholic catechesis. Today Catholics are less likely to think of Jesus in such abstract terms, and renewed attention to the New Testament witnesses has fostered a more biblically oriented appreciation of Jesus as a "real human being," a person like us. Clearly the term *person* has shifted in meaning over the fifteen hundred years since the council of Chalcedon defined that in Christ there is one *person* (Latin *hypostasis*), namely the Son of God, but two *natures*, divine and human, "undivided and unmixed." The key word *hypostasis* has a complex philosophical history: it signifies the substance or individual reality of a thing, as something that "stands up" in reality as a being in its own right. In particular, *hypostasis* was allied to the notion of person, as the most important example of an "upstanding" individual reality. But this is very different from the modern idea of person as outlined in chapter 2, as a center of consciousness, feeling, experience, and relationship. In the modern sense, to speak of Jesus as a human person is simply to affirm his full humanity, "like us in all things but sin." In the context of the debates at Chalcedon, to speak of Jesus as a human person would have been to think of Jesus as a "self-standing" human being, quite independently of his being the Son of God.

The teaching of Chalcedon expanded on the earlier declaration of the Council of Nicea (325) that the Son is "of *one* substance" with God the Father. This technical notion stood in contrast to that of the Son being "of *like* substance" with God the Father. So just as Trent later drew upon thought about "substance" and its properties, these early and decisive councils drew upon philosophical terms to protect the truth of faith in its contest with rival understandings: for example, that Jesus was not fully equal to God, that Jesus was not fully human, that in Jesus humanity and divinity were somehow "mixed." Once again, it is clear that the formulations resolved upon did not explain the truth of faith, but set the parameters for right understanding of the mystery of Christ. Nor did the councils offer a theological articulation of these doctrines. They did not, for example, explain how two "natures" might be found in the one "person"; that was the task of subsequent theological inquiry, notably that of Leontius of Byzantium (480–543), who developed a theology explaining how the human nature of Christ has its being (its *hypostasis*) in the being of the Son or Word of God. As with eucharistic theology, so with Christology, there is ample scope for the development of new theological articulations of the mystery of Christ's identity that will not only be faithful to the decisive profession at Chalcedon but also will offer fresh illumination in changed cultural contexts for people who think in quite different ways.

A final remark concludes this discussion of the role of philosophy in theological inquiry. We have seen how the church has turned to philosophical categories and terms in order to think clearly about the meaning of its profession of faith. As earlier chapters have shown, the data for theological inquiry are the witnesses to faith provided by the Bible and by the tradition and experience of the church. In the course of seeking to understand their faith, Christians may come to a deeper understanding of the original data themselves. Just as new patterns of thought and experience may help to distinguish the *content* of a doctrine from its manner of *formulation,* so a similar refinement of understanding may occur in our reading of the biblical witnesses. In relation to Christology and the theology of the Trinity, for example, we may distinguish the following three stages.[33]

First, there is the study of the biblical witness, the study of how the New Testament portrays the identity and mission of Jesus. For example, stories of Jesus walking on the waves or healing the sick, read in the context of the Old Testament, clearly indicate Jesus' "equality with" God (cf. Phil 2:16, though just what this equality consists in remains to be explained). Likewise, the statement that Jesus was "made Lord" in virtue of God raising him from the dead (Acts 2:36) adds further to a biblical Christology, that is, to the development of a coherent understanding in biblical terms of the person and work of Jesus.

Second, more philosophically informed reflection on the results of this biblical Christology leads to new insights into the nature of God. An understanding of God at work in Jesus and in the sending of the Holy Spirit as both God's Spirit and Christ's Spirit modifies and deepens Christian understanding of God's inner being. In this way, the doctrine of the Trinity, of three "persons" within the one God, develops. This theological articulation concerns what is known as the "immanent Trinity," that is, the inner life of God, to the very limited extent that this can be known. The 1992 *Catechism of the Catholic Church* reminds us that in the ancient church, this understanding of God's own being was theology *(theologia)* properly so called (*CCC* 236).

Third, having deepened our understanding of the being of God as Trinity, we are in a new position to reexamine the biblical data and to reflect again on the mystery of God at work in Jesus through the Holy Spirit. Theological articulation here concerns what is known as the "economic Trinity" *(oikonomia),* the Trinity at work, and it involves a more refined understanding of how God is "at work" in Christ through the Spirit than was available in the initial terms of biblical Christology alone. The *Catechism* remarks:

> *Through the* oikonomia *the* theologia *is revealed to us; but conversely, the* theologia *illuminates the whole* oikonomia. *God's works reveal who he is in himself; the mystery of his inmost being enlightens our understanding of all his works. (CCC 236)*

Explanation and Pluralism

It will be apparent that the two doctrines we have considered, Eucharist and incarnation, were both formulated in the language of "substance metaphysics." The church has judged the metaphysical formulation of doctrine to be necessary in order to safeguard the reality of God and God's action, for these realities need to be considered in those terms that proffer the most fundamental understanding of reality in all its forms, of "being *qua* being." Nevertheless, the church does not endorse any particular philosophical approach as the only one on which theology may draw. This applies as much to the church's moral teaching as to its dogmatic teaching, as Pope John Paul II noted in his encyclical *Veritatis Splendor* when he emphasized that the church "does not intend to impose upon the faithful any particular theological system, still less a philosophical one" (*VS* 29).

The absence of a single "official" theology does not, however, preclude the church from affirming its commitment to certain truths, for example to the reality of Christ's presence in the Eucharist, or to the moral truth that certain kinds of action are inherently disordered, irrespective of an agent's otherwise good intentions (*VS* 80). Yet the absence of an official theology ensures that, even when a truth has been affirmed, it remains for theologians to interpret and develop that truth so as to clarify its content and implications. In this way, new accounts of Christ's eucharistic presence, like new understandings of the foundations of morality, emerge.

Thus, the theologian recognizes that, although *doctrine* cannot be tied to a single theology or philosophy, doctrinal formulation is impossible without relying on some degree of philosophical and theological articulation. Creative theology flourishes in the hermeneutical space between the constraints of doctrine and the strengths and limitations of the chosen mode of articulation. A theology that draws on the insights of a particular philosophy is not thereby committed to that philosophy as such. It may, nevertheless, be distorted by the unavoidable presuppositions, implications, and concomitants of that philosophy. Reliance on certain metaphysical categories, for example, may tend to reduce God to a cosmological principle, just as reliance on critical liberationist categories may tend to reduce the gospel to a program of social and economic reform.

These tensions between doctrine and explanation are reflected in the two documents on liberation theology issued in the 1980s by the Vatican's Congregation for the Doctrine of the Faith. First, there was a critical statement warning against the use of Marxist categories and methods of analysis, that is, warning against the reductive pressure of this philosophy on doctrine. Second, there was the subsequent supportive statement reaffirming the 1980 Synod of Bishops' teaching that working for justice is constitutive of preaching the gospel.[34] Creative theologizing about the demands of social justice will respect the parameters suggested by both of these documents, while seeking the stimulus of fresh readings of the Bible as well as the faith-filled insights of the poor and marginalized.

With respect to using philosophy, therefore, the theologian has great freedom. He or she needs only to remain clearheaded about the strengths and weaknesses of the kind of philosophy employed. Any philosophy that sheds light on aspects of the faith may be drawn upon. In addition to the Marxist insights taken up by liberation theologians, a survey of contemporary Catholic theology reveals the many different philosophical starting points that theologians have adopted, which have in common the desire to go beyond the "physical substance" categories of traditional scholastic theology and philosophy.

There is, first of all, the retrieval of Aquinas's metaphysics over the past hundred years, which demonstrates that the centerpiece of Thomas's thinking was not Aristotle's being as *substance* (as some kind of thing), but rather being as *existence* (designated in Latin by *esse,* the infinitive of the verb "to be"). For Thomas, existence is not a property added on to the substance or essence of a thing, but is the most fundamental "perfection" of any reality. To be a particular kind of thing—that is, to have an essence—is a sign of limitation; it is to be *merely* this or that thing. God, by contrast, is *Ipsum Esse Subsistens*

(Subsistent *Esse* Itself), the perfection of all perfections, the fullness of all reality.

Moreover, in Thomas's account, God should not be thought of as "a supreme being." To put it starkly, if God is *Ipsum Esse Subsistens,* it follows that there is no such thing as *the kind of thing* God is! God is not a kind of thing (God is not *in a genus,* Thomas said), so the endpoint of Thomas's thought is the realization that we *cannot* know God, that we cannot have thoughts that capture the essence of God. We can, Thomas argued, know *that* God is, and *that* God is good, and so on; but the very lines of reasoning by which we reach these conclusions show us why we cannot know *what* is meant by these statements. Should this seem paradoxical, we may recall that in the light of contemporary scientific discoveries, we often know what truths we should affirm without properly understanding what it is we are affirming.

Other recent developments in Thomistic metaphysics give priority to subjectivity rather than existence. The "transcendental Thomism" of Karl Rahner and Bernard Lonergan takes as its starting point the unlimited dynamism of the human person as embodied spirit open to the absolute. With an emphasis on subjectivity rather than substance, and on the dynamism of evolving knowledge rather than static concepts, these thinkers urge that objectivity can only be understood in relation to subjectivity. Reality, above all the reality of God, is not simply "out there" waiting to be looked at. God is always God-for-us. Reality, above all the reality of God, is only known in our engagement with it; therefore, objectivity, in Lonergan's pregnant phrase, is the "fruit of authentic subjectivity." Authentic subjectivity thus becomes a central theological concern: for political and liberationist theologians, authentic subjectivity demands political engagement and action for social justice.

While many traditional Thomists have questioned the validity of the "transcendental" turn, they too have sought to recognize subjectivity by emphasizing the relationality of being *(esse),* such that to be in relationship is a part of the very dynamism of *esse*. Although this relationality is found in limited forms at the subpersonal level, it is with persons that relationality finds its true significance. Moreover, God, on this account, is supremely relational; and human persons can only be rightly understood in terms of their being ordered to relationship with God.[35] Even for traditional Thomists, therefore, a realist metaphysics of being as existence is not incompatible with the affirmation of subjectivity.

Other thinkers have reflected on religious belief and practice from the perspective of the philosophy of language and meaning.[36] They take as their starting point ordered human activity, meaning-making, and the diversity of human practices and cultural forms of life in order to emphasize that religion is not a merely cognitive endeavor but is anchored in practices, sensibility, and cultural forms that must be understood "from within." They suggest that the "transformations of meaning," whereby the world to which human beings belong becomes the world that belongs to them, can be starting points for us as obvious as "primary substances" like plants, animals, and human beings were for Aristotle.[37] On this approach, the real, that is, being *qua* being, is only given to us from within our practices and forms of speech; therefore, God too is only given to us in and through human meaning-making: "The human mind constructs its object, and it is only by means of and through these objectifications that we can know God."[38]

But human meaning-making is not wildly unconstrained. The natural world itself, the basic facts of human nature, and the principles of logic set obvious constraints on what may count as a recognizable human form of life or religious practice. Importantly, nothing in this approach excludes divine order and divine self-communication. Religious practices are not necessarily closed in on themselves. The meaningful ways in which human beings make and shape their world can be, at the same time, a response to the way reality truly is, and to the modes of divine self-communication. Some forms of understanding may be "forced upon us," not as items of sense experience, nor as rational deductions, but "as a whole." As Wittgenstein once suggested:

> *Life can educate one to a belief in God. And* experiences *too are what bring this about; but I don't mean visions and other forms of sense experience which show us the "existence of this being," but for example, sufferings of various sorts. These neither show us God in the way a sense impression shows us an object, nor do they give rise to* conjectures *about him. Experience, thoughts, life can force this concept upon us. So perhaps it is similar to the concept of 'object.'*[39]

Finally, there are theologians taking up the deconstructionist challenge to the very possibility of metaphysics, a challenge particularly associated with French writer Jacques Derrida. Deconstruction, like the broader phenomenon of "postmodernism," primarily seeks to undo the pretensions of "modern" thought, its pretensions to establish all knowledge and truth on a new foundation in autonomous human reason. But the attack of deconstruction on modern thought is clothed in an attack on the entire enterprise of Western thought, whose central assumption of intelligibility, meaning, and ultimate explanation lies at the origins of Western philosophy, theology, and science. The Western assumption that rationality and definite meaning are attainable makes it difficult for us not to think of, and not to think we have thereby comprehended, God as the fullness of being, value, presence, and meaning. There is thus an "onto-theology" implicit in Western thought to the extent that the supreme explanatory metaphysical principle of being is itself regarded as a being (*ontos* means "being" in Greek).

Theologians should welcome the deconstructionist critique of the pretensions of any theology tempted to see itself as a system of thought able to comprehend God. The crucial issue for future theology concerns how it *uses* the concept of God. As Kevin Hart has argued:

> *Deconstruction can make no claim as to the reality or non-reality of God, but will come into operation if I use "God" to ground my account of phenomena; and this is so as long as I regard God as the highest being and the ground of being. Derrida...is concerned with how God has been made to* function *in philosophical and theological systems.*[40]

Deconstruction undermines the use of the concept of God as foundational to a totalizing theological system; it does not undermine the reality of God. What kind of theology, then, may survive the deconstructionist critique? As we have seen, every form of theology is liable to be reductionist, and a metaphysical theology in particular is liable to remain caught in the limits of objectification, of making God into a thing. Some, like Kevin Hart, argue that theology must become "non-metaphysical," perhaps modeled on the "negative theology" associated with the Christian mystical tradition, a theology in which saying what God is *not* is paramount.

We prefer to follow Aquinas in holding that a negative theology that is to be at all meaningful must presuppose some positive theology, however limited. For Thomas the (positive) affirmation that God is, is the prelude to the (negative) realization that we cannot know God. The prospects for this positive metaphysical affirmation need not be as bleak as Derrida claims, provided we abandon the foundationalist and mechanistic assumptions of modern thought, namely, of the world as a great machine with God as its supreme maker. We need to be reminded that God is not *a* being, or *a* meaning, but is Mystery who is love, and who gives to all being the form of relationality and love.[41]

Conclusion: Practice and Coherence

In concluding this chapter, we wish to recall, first, that the demand for rational explanation is both *internal* to forms of life and practice like Christianity, and *external* to those practices insofar as individuals need to make sense of the many forms of life and practice they are engaged in. Although some religious claims are only rationally defensible within the context of Christian theology (for example, the doctrine of the Trinity), Christian belief and practice as a whole raises issues that—from the external perspective—impinge on humankind's various nonreligious beliefs (for example, contemporary cosmology).

But the problem of relating the claims of disparate realms does not arise uniquely in relation to religious belief. As Ingolf Dalferth puts it, "We have to orient ourselves in the multiplicity of forms of life in which we exist. [So in] order to avoid existential schizophrenia we develop second-order beliefs," that is, beliefs about our beliefs, in order to relate coherently the various first-order beliefs we hold in their various contexts.[42] Dalferth continues:

> Rationality is not tied to one form of life only, but neither are our forms of life isolated from each other....Instead there is room for option and argument at every level of life. To live reflectively is to be permanently involved in a process of sorting out the sound beliefs and practices from the unsound ones.[43]

Second, we recall that religious belief is first encountered as something given prior to rational exploration; it is given in tradition, by upbringing, and at times by experiences that "force" the concept of God upon us. The properly philosophical task is not to argue people into belief or to provide a foundation for belief, but to examine the reasons and grounds on which people go on believing.[44] Just as scientific knowledge is inseparable from activity, that is, from engagement with its subject matter, so too religious knowledge is inseparable from engagement with its subject matter, the gracious self-communication of God.

> *Nothing can give substance to our thought of God but an experience which employs our activity in relation to God, where that activity is something other than thought itself; always allowing...that our activity in the matter is passive toward a prior activity of God.*[45]

A philosophically oriented theology with a renewed emphasis on relationality, historicity, and personhood has an important role to play in exploring the assumptions implicit in religious practice. As Austin Farrer puts it:

> *The practice of religion is what brings to life our reasonings about the world's ultimate Cause, and gives reality to them; while on the other side our reasonings about the world give sense and definiteness to a religious faith in God.*[46]

QUESTIONS FOR REFLECTION

1. What are the most influential intellectual currents of thought in your society and culture?

2. What do you judge to be the major intellectual challenges facing Christian belief today?

3. What are the strengths and limitations of all theological explanations?

4. In what ways do you hope that the study of theology will be beneficial for you?

SUGGESTIONS FOR FURTHER READING

- Davies, Brian. *Thinking About God.* London: Geoffrey Chapman, 1985.

- Irwin, Terence. *Classical Thought.* Oxford: Oxford University Press, 1989.

- Ormerod, Neil. *Introducing Contemporary Theologies,* rev. ed. Sydney: E. J. Dwyer, 1997.

- Sokolowski, Robert. *The God of Faith and Reason: Foundations of Christian Theology.* Notre Dame, Ind.: University of Notre Dame Press, 1982.

NOTES

¹Diogenes Allen, *Christian Belief in a Postmodern World* (Louisville, Ky.: Westminster/John Knox, 1989), 16.

²Robert Sokolowski, *The God of Faith and Reason: Foundations of Christian Theology* (Notre Dame, Ind.: University of Notre Dame Press, 1982), 22

³Paul Davies, *The Mind of God: Science and the Search for Ultimate Meaning* (New York and London: Simon & Schuster, 1992), 68. Davies himself is dissatisfied with this account and recognizes the need to ask the further question: where do these laws come from?

⁴Hence there are both similarities and differences (that is, analogy) between the meanings of *cause* in the theological and the scientific contexts. See James F. Ross, "Creation II," in *The Existence and Nature of God,* ed. A. Freddoso (Notre Dame, Ind.: University of Notre Dame Press, 1983), 115–41.

⁵Terence L. Nichols, "Aquinas's Concept of Substantial Form and Modern Science," *International Philosophical Quarterly,* 36 (1996): 311. Nichols points out that the old metaphysics of substantial forms may need to undergo significant development, for example, to accept the existence of "subsidiary forms" within the one substance.

⁶Davies, *The Mind of God,* 92.

⁷Allen, *Christian Belief in a Postmodern World,* 15.

⁸This view explains why it was once customary in Catholic seminaries for the study of philosophy to precede the student's study of theology.

⁹James F. Ross, "On Christian Philosophy: *Una Vera Philosophia?*" *The Monist* 75 (1992): 354–80, at 356.

¹⁰David Coffey, *Believer, Christian, Catholic* (Sydney: Catholic Institute, 1986), 11.

¹¹Allen, *Christian Belief in a Postmodern World,* 144.

¹²Coffey, *Believer, Christian, Catholic,* 11.

¹³Austin Farrer, *Faith and Speculation: An Essay in Philosophical Theology* (Edinburgh: T. & T. Clark, 1988) 12, 15.

¹⁴See Joseph Owens, "Neo-Thomism and Christian Philosophy," in *Thomistic Papers VI,* ed. John F. X. Knasas (Houston, Tex.: Center for

Thomistic Studies, 1994; Notre Dame, Ind.: University of Notre Dame Press, 1994), 29–52.

[15]See Jonathan Barnes, *The Pre-Socratic Philosophers* (London: Routledge & Kegan Paul, 1982), 3–5.

[16]Ingolf Dalferth, *Theology and Philosophy* (Oxford: Blackwell, 1988), 19. The line of thought in this section is much indebted to Dalferth's study.

[17]See Thomas Aquinas, *The Division and Method of the Sciences* (QQ V and VI of his commentary on *The Trinity* of Boethius), 3rd ed., tr. Armand Maurer (Toronto: Pontifical Institute of Medieval Studies, 1963).

[18]The account that follows derives from Dalferth, *Theology and Philosophy,* 35–38.

[19]Dalferth, *Theology and Philosophy,* 36.

[20]Sokolowski, *The God of Faith and Reason,* 32–33.

[21]Nicholas Lash, *Easter in Ordinary: Reflections on Human Experience and the Knowledge of God* (London: SCM Press, 1988; Notre Dame, Ind.: University of Notre Dame Press, 1990), 271.

[22]Charles Taylor, *Human Agency and Language* (Cambridge, U.K.: Cambridge University Press, 1985), 287.

[23]John Henry Newman, *The Via Media of the Anglican Church,* 3rd ed. (London: Basil Montagu Pickering, 1877), xli.

[24]Ibid.

[25]Newman, *A Letter to the Duke of Norfolk,* s. 9, in *The Genius of John Henry Newman,* ed. Ian Ker (Oxford: Clarendon, 1989), 267–68, emphasis added.

[26]Ibid.

[27]Newman, *Via Media,* xlvii.

[28]Council of Trent, Session 13, chapter 4, in *Decrees of the Ecumenical Councils,* ed. Norman P. Tanner (Washington, D.C.: Georgetown University Press, 1990), II:695.

[29]See David Coffey, *Grace: The Gift of the Holy Spirit* (Sydney: Catholic Institute, 1979), 189ff.

[30]C. S. Lewis, "Is Theology Poetry?" reprinted in *Screwtape Proposes a*

Toast and Other Pieces (Glasgow: Fontana, 1965), 52–53.

[31]See Gerard Kelly, *Recognition: Advancing Ecumenical Thinking* (New York: Peter Lang, 1996).

[32]Newman, *A Letter to the Duke of Norfolk,* 268.

[33]See David Coffey, *Deus Trinitas* (forthcoming).

[34]Compare the Congregation for the Doctrine of the Faith's 1984 *Instruction on Certain Aspects of the "Theology of Liberation,"* with its 1986 *Instruction on Christian Freedom.*

[35]See William Norris Clarke, *Explorations in Metaphysics: Being, God, Person* (Notre Dame, Ind.: University of Notre Dame Press, 1994); and David Coffey, *Deus Trinitas,* forthcoming.

[36]See, for example, D. Z. Phillips, *Faith After Foundationalism* (London: Routledge, 1988).

[37]See Cornelius Ernst, *Multiple Echo,* ed. Fergus Kerr and Timothy Radcliffe (London: Darton, Longman & Todd, 1979), 7–27.

[38]Ignace D'Hert, *Wittgenstein's Relevance for Theology,* 2nd ed. (Bern: Peter Lang, 1978), 126.

[39]Ludwig Wittgenstein, *Culture and Value,* ed. G. H. von Wright, with Heikki Nyman, tr. Peter Winch (Oxford: Blackwell, 1980; Chicago: University of Chicago Press, 1984), 86e.

[40]Kevin Hart, *The Trespass of the Sign* (Cambridge, U.K.: Cambridge University Press, 1989), 26, 29.

[41]See David Schindler, "On Meaning and the Death of God in the Academy," *Communio,* 17 (1990): 206.

[42]Dalferth, *Theology and Philosophy,* 7–8.

[43]Dalferth, *Theology and Philosophy,* 8.

[44]Farrer, *Faith and Speculation,* 2.

[45]Farrer, *Faith and Speculation,* 28.

[46]Austin Farrer, *God Is Not Dead* (New York: Morehouse & Barlow, 1966), 70.

Chapter Six

UNITING FAITH AND THE MORAL LIFE

> Morality is a necessary foundation of our humanity; it ensures that our lives and our interactions with the world around us are founded on what is "truly good" for ourselves and others. The task of moral theology is to explore how Christian faith can shape our conception of what is truly good and our endeavors to live according to that good.

Modern market-driven societies are geared to produce goods and to satisfy wants as efficiently as possible. Sometimes this can seem an exclusive preoccupation. Seamus Heaney, the Nobel Prize-winning Irish poet, observes of contemporary attitudes:

> ....*My people think money*
> *And talk weather. Oil rigs lull their future*
> *On single acquisitive stems..........*[1]

Acquisitiveness implies a dedicated pursuit of one's own desires, unimpeded by any other consideration. Yet if we want to introduce the topic of morality into our discussion, it has to be as some such "other consideration," because it will directly focus on those very wants we are bent on fulfilling. For morality is about judging whether this or that desire is truly good, or whether it is, in fact, bad, because its pursuit will undermine what is truly good for ourselves and others.

Questions of morality will arise for us only when we put concerns about profit, productivity, and strategy aside for a moment and become sensitive to the potential good or harmful effects our behavior may have

145

on the world around us. Is it right for us to break a promise simply because something more exciting has come along? Should we offer assistance, when in a position to do so, to someone in need? Is it ever right to take advantage of others, for example, by paying them less than they are owed in wages? Should we care about the environment? To raise such questions at all is to be concerned about the potential richness of the life we share with others: Are such attributes as integrity, respect for rights, honesty, truthfulness, and compassion necessary to guarantee a truly human quality in our lives? Do we see that manipulation, exploitation, discrimination, and cruelty are destructive of our relationships with others? These are inescapable issues for any thinking human being, even if eventually we decide to disregard them, because these issues are about the ramifications, often serious, that our decisions and actions have on the world around us. The answers and responses we give to these issues will contribute to our developing vision of what it is to be truly human and will also determine the kind of person we ourselves become through our choices.

While it may be clear that all of the questions raised above are genuinely human questions, it may be less obvious that they are theological questions. If we are to establish theology's right to be involved in such questions, we need to call to mind the five principles that have emerged from the previous chapters of this book: (1) theology is a human activity that excludes nothing human from its ambit; (2) theology is inseparable from the human desire to find meaning and the "more" in life; (3) the faith that underpins theology is a response to God's self-communication in Jesus Christ, a revelation that is directed toward fulfilling our God-given longing for the "more"; (4) this revelation lives on in a community of faith and is mediated by the community's tradition, of which the Bible is a paradigmatic expression; and (5) in the ongoing quest to appropriate and to respond to God's self-communication, the Christian community makes use of all the tools of understanding that the human genius has produced. All of this means that a theology that claimed to be uninterested in the moral issues affecting the quality of human existence would be an inauthentic theology.

Since moral issues are at the heart of the human, authentic theology cannot separate itself from the human struggle to discern how to live well. Theology cannot provide prepackaged solutions that absolve us from the struggle to find what is right and good. Indeed, theology manifests itself as a human activity by its cooperation with the processes by which humans come to know and decide; among these processes is our need to learn how to become moral beings.

Learning To Be Moral

Moral standards do not suddenly appear out of nowhere. They are already embedded in the way of life we are born into, in its attitudes, values, and practices. Family, culture, education, the church, and our own growing experience are all possible sources for our moral learning. Moral standards will be handed on to us in role models, customs, stories, and explicit moral teaching. We appropriate them in our own learning to be sensitive to the needs and feelings of others.

It is possible, of course, for a person to learn nothing, or next to nothing, of such things. The result is a person who is "amoral," that is, unconcerned about others, entirely unscrupulous, or even worse, vicious. More often, however, we find ourselves caught somewhere in between, struggling to hold on to standards, but prey to contradictory urges and easily tempted to follow the line of least resistance. Contemporary society with its divergent views and powerful media influences does not make the matter any easier. We find our moral authorities in conflict: parents, church leaders, peer groups, and media figures are all sometimes at odds with one another, creating further confusion in our minds as we attempt to give some direction to our lives.

One essential prerequisite in the assumption of responsibility for our actions is that we must *want* to be moral in the first place. This means seeing that the whole point of morality is the quality of our lives. If we have not picked this up from our moral education, we are not yet at first base. This is not just a matter of the mind, but, even more so, of our feelings and powers of imagination. The English novelist Julian Barnes makes the point very tellingly:

> *What else can love do? If we're selling it, we'd better point out that it's a starting-point for civic virtue. You can't love someone without imaginative sympathy, without beginning to see the world from another point of view. You can't be a good lover, a good artist or a good politician without this capacity (you can get away with it, but that's not what I mean).*[2]

"First base," then, means finding for ourselves sources of motivation that will enable us to respond morally to the world around us. Certainly, principles, moral concepts, rules, and the many other things gained from our moral education will be indispensable for perceiving and assessing what is morally relevant in the situations we must face. But above all, we will need something to counter the bias, prejudice, insensitivity, and blindness that will certainly prevent us, if unchecked, from responding imaginatively to the needs and feelings of those others who are affected by our actions.

What must be jealously safeguarded at this point is the integrity of our own freedom of choice. *Conscience* is our inviolable moral space of decision-making where we must assume responsibility for what we do or—often unremarked, but sometimes just as significant—for what we do not do. There we must judge according to our own lights. We have a duty to "form" our conscience by taking whatever care is required to ensure that we are adequately informed and in a position to make our judgment of conscience. Although this will not guarantee that what we decide to do will truly be the right thing in the circumstances, nevertheless, it must be recognized that, subjectively, our conscience is the final arbiter of our moral goodness or badness: morally good, if we have been conscientious in forming and following conscience; morally bad, if we have been negligent or acted against it. It is always necessary to consult one's conscience in these matters, but it is also all that can be reasonably demanded of us: we have decided according to the best of our ability. Respect for conscience, then, protects our capacity to give direction to our lives for good or ill. This respect found full expression in *Gaudium et Spes,* the Second Vatican Council's Pastoral Constitution on the Church in the Modern World:

> *Their conscience is people's most secret core, and their sanctuary. There they are alone with God whose voice echoes in their depths. By conscience, in a wonderful way, that law is made known which is fulfilled in the love of God and of one's neighbor. Through loyalty to conscience, Christians are joined to others in the search for truth and for the right solution to so many moral problems which arise both in the life of individuals and from social relationships. (GS 16)*

Within this space of conscience, we struggle to grow in humanity and to define the kind of persons we will be. It is thus the place of moral commitment and accountability. At the same time, as the statement from the council indicates, following conscience, whatever our beliefs, grounds our personal response to God in the fabric of our lives. For our moral response to others takes us beyond the narrow confines of our own interests to relate us to what is Other than ourselves, even if we are unable to name that Other in its fullness. Morality opens up within our own individual experience the possibility of questions about our own personal destiny and that of those we love, and about the ultimate fate of all moral endeavors. It is this transcendent dimension of our moral striving that religion seeks to name and to express. The task of theology is to reflect on this religious basis and to articulate it in terms of the rich variety of human experience, in particular, as it concerns us in this chapter, our experience of the moral demands made on us.

The Witness of Scripture

From the beginning, the Judaeo–Christian religion has understood faith and moral life to be inseparable. For example, Hosea, active as a prophet in the troubled years leading up to the fall of Samaria to the invading Assyrian forces in 722 B.C.E., testifies to the havoc wreaked in the land by the violation of the covenant with Yahweh. The widespread abandonment of the religious virtues of faithfulness and loyalty is linked with the breakdown of family life, with atrocities and civil anarchy, resulting in the devastation of the fragile order of their agrarian world. People could see the evidence all around them, as the prophet points out:

> *Hear the word of the Lord,*
> *O people of Israel;*
> *for the Lord has an indictment*
> *against the inhabitants of the land*
>
> *There is no faithfulness or loyalty,*
> *and no knowledge of God in the land.*
> *Swearing, lying, and murder,*
> *and stealing and adultery break out;*
> *bloodshed follows bloodshed.*
>
> *Therefore the land mourns,*
> *and all who live in it languish;*
> *together with the wild animals*
> *and the birds of the air,*
> *even the fish of the sea are perishing. (Hos 4:1–3)*

This link between religion and life is characteristic of the scriptures as a whole, but it is not a connection that is simply taken for granted. The book of Ecclesiastes, written some five hundred years after Hosea in a time of questioning occasioned by Israel's first contacts with Greek civilization, radically reexamines the traditional presupposition that God rewards good and punishes evil, a belief characteristic of times of cultural stability and seclusion, but out of step in a period of political turmoil and cultural exchange. No final answer or secure salvation is available in the world as we know it, according to Ecclesiastes. God is a mystery beyond human grasp; furthermore, the hard facts of unchecked evil belie all facile answers—an enduring lesson for all ages that theology should never bypass the data of human experience. For Ecclesiastes, wisdom must be sought, but at its heart must remain an acknowledgment of a mystery that is ever liable to contradict our deepest presuppositions and our fondest expectations:

> *When I applied my mind to know wisdom, and to see the business that is done on earth, how one's eyes see sleep neither day nor night, then I saw all the work of God, that no one can find out what is happening under the sun. However much they may toil in seeking, they will not find it out; even though those who are wise claim to know, they cannot find it out. (Eccl 8:16–17)*

Ecclesiastes' admonition is equally valid for the New Testament era. As we have already seen in chapter 3, Christians believe that in Jesus, the mystery of God is uniquely manifested in human history, not as an end, but as a new beginning to the search for what is truly good. The full reality and challenge of this revelation of God in the life and ministry of Jesus is in danger of being lost if we allow Jesus to be domesticated by our late-twentieth-century consumer interests. Jesus' words and actions manifest to us the unpredictability of the mystery of God, ever poised, as it is, to confound our most settled presuppositions and self-interested concerns. A complete overturning of one's life is demanded (Mk 1:15); Jesus' contemporaries are shocked by his eating with tax collectors and sinners (Lk 5:30–32); devils are cast out (Lk 4:40–41); wisdom is revealed not to the wise but to little ones (Mt 11:25–27); Jesus proclaims that the kingdom belongs to the poor, hungry, sorrowful, and persecuted (Lk 6:20–23); the law is radicalized in terms of forgiveness of enemies and compassion (Lk 6); his followers are taught that humble service must replace rank and dominance (Mk 10:41–45). The list continues, the mystery reaching its climax in Jesus' death as a criminal on the cross and in his resurrection.

The full reality of the gospel's engagement with our lives across the centuries, even though historical and social conditions are dramatically altered, is captured by the scriptures as the gift of the Spirit of Christ received in faith:

> *But the Advocate, the Holy Spirit, whom the Father will send in my name, will teach you everything, and remind you of all that I have said to you. (Jn 14:26)*

For Christians, the Spirit of Christ is a reality of human history, a liberating and empowering experience that was expressed in a multitude of terms as the early disciples strove to do justice to this new quality of life that had overtaken them: "new creation" (2 Cor 5:17–19); "rebirth" (Jn 3:3–8); freedom "from the law of sin and death" (Rom 8:2), "love, joy, peace, patience, kindness, generosity, faithfulness, gentleness, and self-control" (Gal 5:22), to mention only a few. For their moral lives, it was experienced, above all, as a freedom from the stultifying effects of sin, superstition, and enmity, which had disabled them both personally and in their relationships with the world around them. Their new experience was an openness to God's future and to the opportunities it unlocked for the fulfillment of all creation (Rom 8:18–25). To express the full impact of their new faith on their moral lives, they took a little-used Greek word, *agapē,* originally meaning 'kindly concern,' and made it the vehicle to express the mystery of God engaging and transforming their lives at the most basic level of their concrete desires and interactions with each other:

> *Love one another* as *I have loved you. No one has greater love than this, to lay down one's life for one's friends. (Jn 15:12–13)*

This impact is dramatically captured in the "as" of the above quotation, which brings the whole mystery of God revealed in the *agapē* of Jesus to bear upon believers' attempts to relate to the world around them. Thus, the witness of scripture indicates clearly the direction Christian morality needs to travel: the path of reconciliation, compassion, and practical concern in imitation of Jesus. This is never presented as the foreclosure of the search for what is truly good, but is left expansively open to imaginatively embrace "whatever is true, whatever is honorable, whatever is just, whatever is pure, whatever is pleasing, whatever is commendable"(Phil 4:8). It becomes the task of every Christian to translate this mystery manifested in Jesus into the concrete conditions of life in the world.

Historical Development

Religious beliefs and ethics can each be said to have their own languages in the sense that they have their own particular points of reference—on the one hand, God, and on the other, human good—each with its own principles and logical processes of articulation. This articulation of Christian standards to guide conduct always occurs, like the exercise of theology in general, in a particular social context, using whatever cultural resources are available. The task of translation from faith to ethics, therefore, is perceived and undertaken in different ways, corresponding to the new contexts experienced by the Christian community down through the ages. Prevailing thought patterns—especially ways of understanding what it is to be human—political and economic infrastructures, customs, and the kind of moral issues that must be faced (such as nuclear warfare or genetic engineering in today's world) will all exert their influence on that task.

In the Graeco-Roman culture into which the early church was almost immediately thrust, prevailing philosophical ideas relating to such things as the rule of reason over emotions and a cosmic order underpinning the universe, and current moral terms, such as the cardinal virtues of justice, temperance, fortitude, and prudence, were quickly adopted and incorporated into a growing Christian vocabulary. Scripture, as we have already seen, is the primary source for Christian theology. In this early period, however, rather than a reflective translation from faith to ethics, scripture itself was directly mined for concrete indications of what was or was not morally right for a Christian.

Though a rather haphazard and piecemeal method in itself because of its selectivity and lack of systematic application of scriptural texts, this translation from faith to ethics achieved its greatest expression in the work of St. Augustine, whose moral teaching was established on the twin beliefs that the human soul was made for God and that grace was absolutely necessary to attain that end. For Augustine, the gift of the

Holy Spirit is the indwelling of charity in the soul as the love of God above all things; charity then becomes the rule governing all human loves and ordering them rightly to God. The content of morality was taken to be provided by the divine commands discovered in revelation, a selective process that, in fact, tended to be guided by Augustine's pessimistic view of human capabilities. A good example of this method is provided by Augustine's redefinition of the four principal Graeco-Roman virtues in terms of charity:

> *As to virtue leading us to a happy life, I hold virtue to be nothing else than perfect love of God. For the fourfold division of virtue I regard as taken from four forms of love...temperance as love giving itself entirely to that which is loved; fortitude is love readily bearing all things for the sake of the beloved object; justice is love serving only the loved object, and therefore ruling rightly; prudence is love distinguishing with sagacity between what hinders it and what helps it.*[3]

During the Middle Ages, Western society grew more complex politically and economically with the expansion of trade, enabled by the new routes opened up by adventurers such as Marco Polo (c. 1254–1324) and the gradual emergence of the nation-state. The driving force of the age was the burgeoning desire to achieve a greater rational control over human affairs, especially the affairs of state. The church had accumulated a thousand years of theological baggage—some priceless, much past its use-by date, and all of it requiring to be made more portable to meet the new demands of reason. A good example of the need for such revision can be seen in the history of natural law.

Natural law was an ethical theory that had come down to medieval thinkers from classical Graeco-Roman Stoic philosophy. It grounded ethics in an "order" that they believed underpinned the universe and governed human affairs. Taken over and developed by successive generations of theologians, and employing the new logical skills developed by such thinkers as Peter Abelard (1079–1142), natural law became the vehicle for synthesizing a reorganized theology with a new appreciation of human reason. At its best, in the hands of a skilled moralist such as St. Thomas Aquinas, natural law is an insightful and creative synthesis of traditional wisdom with the emerging understanding of a human reality considered in its own right, a dimension that tended to be obscured in Augustine by the overwhelming emphasis placed on love of God above all things.

Aquinas grafted into Augustine's primacy of charity an ordered understanding of human nature, an attention to the needs and desires belonging to human existence as such, which is the true source for moral principles and the processes of practical reasoning. This "order" is conceived in the cultural terms available to Aquinas, as must always be the case in any age, for there is no God's eye view that is above history and culture. Accordingly, such features as his prescientific biological knowledge regarding procreation, a subordinate role for women, and excessive ecclesial claims must be treated cautiously but should not be allowed to undermine his achievement. Nature, according to Aquinas, is grounded in God's goodness; therefore, what reason is able to discover as essential elements in human existence are to be taken as the vital clues for achieving human happiness. Aquinas found that self-preservation, procreation, and participation in society form an interrelated set of basic human goods, within the context of which all other goods necessary for human fulfillment were to be situated. Practical reason sets out to harmonize this complex of goods, subordinating lower to higher as required, in ever more particular applications to the changing circumstances of the world. It is a flexible system, sensitive to the subtleties of moral language and designed to preserve a rational structure and integrity within moral reasoning, but supplemented when necessary, due to human inadequacy, by the divine law found in the scriptures.

The following quotation from an article in which Thomas Aquinas asks, "Should we love one neighbor more than another?" (a question to which Augustine answered, "No, we should love all neighbors equally") demonstrates how skillfully Thomas incorporated—albeit within the medieval worldview with its prescientific beliefs—the everyday experience of degrees of closeness to others into his understanding of the different moral demands of charity:

> Charity's love, which is an inclination of grace, is no less well-ordered than natural love, which is an inclination of nature, for both are works of divine wisdom. Now observe that, in the physical world, natural tendencies are proportioned to the actions or movements which accord with the various natures of things; for example, earth has a greater gravitational tendency than water, because its nature is to be under water. Therefore, it must also be the case that the tendency which grace has, the affection of charity, in other words, should also be proportionate to the occasion,

so that our affection for those towards whom we ought to show
more kindness is more intense than it is for others.[4]

While Aquinas's theology manifests the best possible usage of the natural law, not all who followed him were as creative or as positive. At its worst, natural law theory, preoccupied as it was with the canonical requirements laid down by the Council of Trent for the hearing of confessions—for example, that an integral confession must include the number and kind of mortal sins committed—became excessively legalistic and sin-focused, degenerating into an over-systematized set of moral principles that remained impervious to all outside influences, even to scripture, to other theological disciplines, and certainly to the emerging human sciences. The Second Vatican Council, aware of this situation, recognized, in *Optatam Totius,* the Decree on Priestly Formation, that there was a need for a renewal of Catholic moral theology:

> *In like manner the other theological subjects should be renewed*
> *through a more living contact with the mystery of Christ and the*
> *history of salvation. Special care is to be taken for the improve-*
> *ment of moral theology. Its scientific presentation, drawing more*
> *fully on the teaching of holy scripture, should highlight the lofty*
> *vocation of the Christian faithful and their obligation to bring*
> *forth fruit in charity for the life of the world. (OT 16)*

In the years following the council, two major views emerged within Catholic theology on the way faith and morality should be integrated.[5] One opinion focused on the "rationality" of Christian ethics, a heritage of the natural law tradition that some theologians thought should be preserved. Ethics, they insisted, is about the human good: whatever is authentically human, therefore, is morally good. In principle, at least, dialogue about that good should be open to all people of good will, whether Christian or not. This means that only reasons concerned with human well-being should be allowed in such moral debate. The role of faith, then, is not to colonize the good with religious interpretations that would exclude others, but to provide sources of motivation to live morally and to support morality by its religious teaching. The content of morality, they concluded, was a sphere in its own right, the logical autonomy of which had to be respected by all parties, including religion.

The other opinion considered religion to be more than simply motivation and context for ethics: faith, they believed, also had an impact on the *content* of morality. Christ is the ultimate norm of Christian ethics; therefore, faith contains values and meanings that do not exist for the non-Christian. Such values and meanings, however, profoundly alter what the Christian understands concerning human well-being, thus creating an ethic that is specifically Christian in content and hence unavailable to those who do not share that faith.

At this point, the theological debate reaches an impasse. Two facts stand out. First, Judaeo-Christianity has always considered religion and morality to be inseparably linked—love and justice, the Bible reminds us from first to last, must be the basic expression of religious faith and worship. Second, we live today in secular societies within which people of many faiths (and none at all) must endeavor to achieve some basic moral consensus if such societies are to survive and prosper. The debate, therefore, is not abstract and irrelevant, but touches intimately the daily practice of our faith in a modern pluralist society. Perhaps a way out of this impasse can be found if the issue is examined in more concrete detail.

Faith and Ethics

How do we determine in practice what is truly good? We want many things, some of them we want badly. Only some of them would we consider, in our honest moments, things we truly need. Others, we might admit if pressed, we could do without. Of the rest, we would probably find it difficult to decide one way or another. In earlier ages such issues would have been sorted out for people, for the most part, whether they conformed or not, by the dominant belief system of their culture. Without serious competitors, some belief system would have provided basic notions of what it regarded as good or bad, the details being filled out by "taboo," tradition, or local custom. Crises may have occurred at times of transition, but consensus would be restored once a new worldview was in place.

In our age, we are far more conscious of history and cultural diversity, and of the highly persuasive influences that vie for our allegiance. The calamities of the twentieth century have also made us deeply suspicious of the destructive potential of authoritative answers, such as the myths of the "master race," the "classless society," or their religious equivalents.

As problematic as the question of the truly good may be in modern society, however, it cannot be jettisoned as unnecessary baggage that hinders our enjoyment of life. Decisions about the truly good are an inseparable part of every choice that is made. Often we say, "This is good for me. I want it!" But we can also ask, What about my family? Others? The environment? If I choose my good and in so doing harm myself or others, I have already decided where I stand in relation to the truly good: such goods as family, friendship, justice, or compassion are then sidelined; I have thus chosen a "flat earth" view of the good, ruling out of my life any fuller vision of the world.

Granted, then, that we are willing to leave the flat earth view behind and to sail into the waters of morality, in which direction should we head? A good start will be made if we realize at the outset that there is a real sense in which these waters are "uncharted." The truly good is not an abstract concept but a historical reality, always shifting with the winds of historical and cultural change. Basic human needs do remain constant, a truth seized on by natural law theory, but precisely how these needs are perceived and satisfied will depend on the conditions of time and place.

A second important compass bearing to note is that a person does not have to be religious to have an opinion about "the good." Many people are moral without being religious. If a religious version of the good is put forward, the question of whether it is truly good is always an open possibility. It seems clear, therefore, that we do need to recognize, at least as a basis, a restricted sense of morality, with its own rationale and reasons to do with human well-being, that is logically distinct from other areas, including religion. For Christians, religion will include the moral good, respecting its integrity as a distinct human concern, but will reach beyond it to the Source of the Good as the Mystery that responds to our ultimate questions of life and death. This position, so far, safeguards the possibility of all people of good will contributing to rational moral discussion as required in a pluralist society, but leaves unresolved the question of how they can be productively related to one another.

What must also be retained is the important insight of the other side of the debate: that faith can be a God-given resource for discovering what is truly good. To permit a "direct" contribution of faith to morality, however, would destroy the integrity of moral reasoning. By directly inserting statements such as "God commands this" or "Scripture teaches that" into a moral discussion, we undermine its logical processes, when what we most need to realize is that the real contribution to the debate lies rather in seeking the reasons *why* this or that might be commanded or taught in the scriptures.

Faith is able to influence the content of morality, but its contribution must be indirect, rather than direct. God's revelation addresses all that we are, especially our moral life, but at the same time, it respects our reality as human beings. Our response in faith is enabled by grace, but the integrity of conscience and of the moral reasoning process remains intact.

More, however, than "motivation" and "context" is involved. Our religious experience is capable of releasing new perceptions and standards that will affect our appreciation of what it is to be fully human. A myriad of possible points of contact exist between the quality of our relationship with God revealed in Christ and our endeavors to preserve true humanity in our interactions with our neighbor. What are the implications of the parable of the Good Samaritan (Lk 10:29–37) or Jesus' prohibition of divorce (Mt 5:27–32) or Paul's statement that "there is no longer Jew or Greek...slave or free...male and female; for all of you are one in Christ Jesus" (Gal 3:28) for our contemporary understanding of the truly good? They certainly provide an impetus for Christians to place a high value on faithfulness in marriage, compassion for the needy, and respect for each and every person, regardless of race, status, or gender, all of which are distinctive features of any authentically Christian ethic. Morality must still articulate its own reasons and develop them into a coherent system, but it will do so, in the case of Christian morality, in the direction indicated by faith.

Our faith and morality emerge together from the tradition of the church as it faithfully hands on from generation to generation, in ever-changing circumstances, what has been committed to it in Jesus. This faith, in the words of the council's Dogmatic Constitution on Divine Revelation, *Dei Verbum,* is entrusted to the church as a whole. But the teaching authority, as we have seen in chapter 1, has a particular responsibility for ensuring the authenticity of the tradition:

> *The task of giving an authentic interpretation of the word of God, whether in its written form or in the form of tradition, has been entrusted to the living teaching office of the Church alone. Its authority in this matter is exercised in the name of Jesus Christ. The*

*magisterium is not superior to the word of God, but is rather its ser-
vant. It teaches only what has been handed on to it. At the divine
command and with the help of the Holy Spirit, it listens to this
devoutly, guards it reverently and expounds it faithfully. (DV 10)*

This means that the magisterium is responsible for the safeguarding of the moral foundation of Christian "faith working through love"
(Gal 5:6). Magisterial teaching can play its proper role in the development of the tradition only when there is loyal adherence to it by the
members of the church who must apply it in the circumstances of a
changing world. The *Catechism of the Catholic Church* explains in
greater detail the role of the magisterium in the life of the church:

The Magisterium of the Pastors of the Church *in moral matters is
ordinarily exercised in catechesis and preaching, with the help of
the works of theologians and spiritual authors. Thus from generation to generation, under the aegis and vigilance of the pastors,
the "deposit" of Christian moral teaching has been handed on, a
deposit composed of a characteristic body of rules, commandments, and virtues proceeding from faith in Christ and animated
by charity. Alongside the Creed and the Our Father, the basis for
this catechesis has traditionally been the Decalogue which sets
out the principles of moral life valid for all men* [sic]. *(CCC 2033)*

Rules, commandments, and teachings on virtue and vice are the
ways that moral wisdom is handed on from one generation to another in
the church. They encapsulate what the church is able to offer its members for the formation of an authentically Christian conscience. In
some cases, according to the Catholic Church's teaching, they indicate
acts that should never be done no matter what the circumstances, for
example, killing the innocent or torture.[6] Rules, however, should not be
thought of as a substitute for our own moral discernment, prayerful
reflection, or conscientious application of moral wisdom to the changing conditions of daily life. Principles and rules contribute the moral
vocabulary that is essential if we are to be able to take account of all the
relevant moral features of the situations we face. Without the concepts
they provide of such things as rights, without the descriptions they
enable of different cases of injustice—for example, murder, sexual
abuse, theft, discrimination—and without the recommendations they
promote of promise keeping, truth telling, and fidelity, we would not be

able to recognize these features in our relationships with one another. Yet we must remember that rules and principles direct us toward a truly human response to the real needs and feelings of others, which is the whole point of moral obligation. The nineteenth-century English author George Eliot provides a striking warning against misunderstanding what morality is truly about:

> *All people of broad strong sense have an instinctive repugnance to the men of maxims; because such people early discern that the mysterious complexity of our life is not to be embraced by maxims, and that to lace ourselves up in formulas of that sort is to repress all the divine prompting and inspirations that spring from growing insight and sympathy. And the man of maxims is the popular representative of the minds that are guided in their moral judgment solely by general rules, thinking that these will lead them to justice by a ready-made method, without the trouble of exerting patience, discrimination, impartiality, without any care to assure themselves whether they have the insight that comes from a hardly-earned estimate of temptation, or from a life vivid and intense enough to have created a wide fellow-feeling with all that is human.[7]*

A mechanical application of general rules is therefore both an abdication of responsibility and a practice that is potentially dangerous to those affected by it, because it is prone to misrepresent their real needs and feelings. Each moral judgment should be a sensitive determination of where the true good lies in these particular circumstances. It is this determination that also allows traditional moral wisdom to be challenged and rejuvenated. It is there that the voices of victims of new injustices may be heard, where new sensitivities have the opportunity to emerge, and where faith is allowed to call us prophetically to new levels of compassion and service. A good example of such a reorganization of our current thinking is the recent introduction of a concept of "discrimination" on such grounds as gender, race, religion, or sexual preference into our moral vocabulary. Forms of pain, previously suppressed, have now been allowed to register in our moral consciousness, thus creating new sensitivities to what is truly good. Without such renewal, a moral system becomes itself a form of oppression. The final test of the relationship of our faith to our moral life can only be, therefore, its effectiveness in keeping our minds and hearts open to the real needs of our neighbors and of ourselves.

Faith and Moral Living

Morality requires us to mesh our wants with those of others, to recognize that on some occasions at least, the good of others should take precedence over our own preferences. In order to be able to do this, a certain level of moral development needs to have been attained. Morality requires such things as the ability to recognize the potential good or harm, whether to ourselves or to others, that is at stake in some action we contemplate doing; the ability to perceive possible alternatives to our immediate desires (lest our own wants overwhelm us); and the availability, in the first place, of the motivation that moves us to be concerned about the true good of ourselves and of others. We are not long on such a moral path, however, before we are brought face to face with our own shortcomings: selfishness, prejudice, callousness, and spite, to mention only a few, are likely, at some time or other, if not persistently, to become character traits that mar our relationships with others. We must acknowledge with regret that we do hurt ourselves and others by at least some, if not many, of the things we do or fail to do.

It is at this deep-seated level of our moral selves that faith has most to offer us. The God revealed to us in Jesus is a compassionate, reconciling, and affirming God. Faith, with its vision and power to free us, is able to open up within our experience a "space" for others. Instead of being totally identified with our own wants and interests, the symbols, narratives, and teachings of faith are able to remold our patterns of desiring so that our alternatives for choice are expanded and new possibilities of reaching out to others, especially to their needs, are offered to us. Within the living reality of our faith, such powerful features as the prophets' defense of justice for the poor, the parable of the Good Samaritan, and Jesus' own moral practice, especially his passion and death, are at work in our lives to counter our self-serving tendencies, to sustain us with forgiveness and hope, to expand our sympathies, and to lead us to respond to the misfortunes of others.

This process is not, of course, without its obstacles. A misinformed faith can trap us either in devotionalism, where our own personal salvation and the interior life of the church become paramount, or in one of the many aberrant forms of fanaticism, where we misconceive what is "good." Affluence can dull our sensitivities and redirect all our efforts back to our own comfort and convenience. The media can offer fashionable stereotypes of "success" that beguile our imagination and truncate our sense of the good. Ideologies such as capitalism, individualism, and materialism present their own versions of morality, at odds with the message of the gospel. What is at stake here is the kind of person we are to become by our choices and actions. Our moral character is the end product of what we do or do not do, in the sense that our concrete choices determine the fundamental orientation of our lives for good or for ill. Pope John Paul II's encyclical letter on the church's moral teaching, *Veritatis Splendor,* issued in 1993, brings out the full reality involved:

> *It has been rightly pointed out that freedom is not only the choice of one or another particular action; it is also, within that choice, a decision about oneself and a setting of one's own life for or against the Good, for or against the Truth, and ultimately for or against God. (VS 65)*

Nor is this something we can take or leave as we please. What we become is the way we relate to others, the way we see the world, the way we respond to the situations we face, and the way we are within ourselves. Justice, compassion, love, fidelity, and the other virtues enable us to see the world in terms of people's rights, needs, feelings, and well-founded expectations of us, and, generally, to see the world as peopled by others equal to ourselves and deserving of our respect. Without such a language of virtue (and vice), we will not be aware of these things in the world around us, nor is there any possibility that they could even form part of our lives and relationships.

The moral world is potentially a rich world, where the truly good for oneself and others may flourish and where mutually enhancing relationships are possible. It is, however, a world profoundly at risk from changes both within and without. Faith is able to liberate morality from the vacuum of unbelief, to allow it to breathe the atmosphere of God's kingdom, which promises the fulfillment of our moral efforts for a better world, even in the face of evil and the vicissitudes of history, and to provide a hope that can sustain us despite our moral weakness and many failures. In Christ, faith has both a reservoir of moral insights to provide direction in our search for the truly good and, even more crucially, the pardon and healing that morality itself is unable to provide. Christianity is above all, then, not simply a system of beliefs, but a way of being with others, a way of living one's life in the world.

QUESTIONS FOR REFLECTION

1. What contribution do moral standards make to our relationships with the world around us?

2. How is Christian faith able to influence our moral thinking?

3. What is faith able to offer our relationships with others?

4. Which moral standards are particularly associated with Christian faith?

SUGGESTIONS FOR FURTHER READING

- Hodge, Robert. *What's Conscience For?* Middlegreen: St. Paul Publications, 1995.

- Kelly, Kevin T. *New Directions in Moral Theology.* London: Geoffrey Chapman, 1992.

- Moran, Gabriel. *A Grammar of Responsibility.* New York: Crossroad, 1996.

- Porter, Jean. *Moral Action and Christian Ethics.* Cambridge, U.K.: Cambridge University Press, 1995.

NOTES

[1]Seamus Heaney, "Triptych," in *New Selected Poems, 1966–1987* (London: Faber & Faber, 1990; New York: Farrar, Strauss and Giroux, 1990), 94.

[2]Julian Barnes, *A History of the World in 10½ Chapters* (London: Picador, 1989; New York: Knopf, 1989), 243.

[3]"Of the Morals of the Catholic Church" 15, in *The Nicene and Post-Nicene Fathers* (Grand Rapids, Mich.: Eerdmans, 1979), IV:48.

[4]*Summa Theologiae* 2a 2ae, 26.6.

[5]For an excellent account of this debate, see Vincent MacNamara, *Faith and Ethics* (Dublin: Gill & MacMillan, 1985).

[6]See *Veritatis Splendor* 79–83, a document issued in 1993 by Pope John Paul II on Catholic morality; and *Evangelium Vitae* 52–77, a document issued in 1995 by Pope John Paul II in defense of the sanctity of human life.

[7]George Eliot, *The Mill on the Floss* (London: Penguin Classics, 1979), 628.

Chapter Seven

TESTED BY PRACTICE

This chapter will explore the relationship between theological understanding and action in the world. We will describe and evaluate different models of theology in practice and, by using a concrete pastoral example, we will illustrate how these approaches operate.

Imagine that in the community in which you live there is a debate going on about whether enough is being done to aid refugees who have come to settle in your country. Does this debate have anything to do with you? More particularly, does this debate have anything to do with you as a person of faith? There may be many voices heard during this debate, voices that range from radio's "shock jocks" complaining that the refugees have been pampered, to members of advocacy groups reminding the government that it has a responsibility to assist the refugees. But is there a voice from those who claim that at the center of their lives is the gospel of Jesus Christ?

It should be clear from this book's presentation of the human person as social, its analysis of the purpose of God's self-revelation, and its discussion of the moral life as a search for truth and integrity in the light of faith, that the issue of the refugees cannot be excluded from the concerns of faith. More explicitly, the issues associated with their treatment cannot be excluded from the concerns of theology, especially of a theology shaped by faith in God's self-communication in Jesus Christ. What needs to be identified, however, is how people of faith can develop, and act upon, a response to the situation of the refugees. In other words, what needs to be identified is how we are to do theology in practice.

While it is undeniable that there have been moments in its history when theology became absorbed in abstractions, it is also true that the conviction that theology has a practical orientation, that faith is inseparable from action in the world, has been an essential element of the richest periods in the annals of theology.

Contemporary theology too is aware that the need to respect the practical orientation of theology means that criteria based on intellectual rigor and consistency cannot be the only ones we use to test the validity of a theology. We have emphasized throughout this book that intellectual rigor and consistency make their greatest contribution when they remain united to, rather than elevated above, the imperative that theology must connect faith and life.

It could be argued that the search for the best way to connect faith and life has yielded more diversity than can be found in any other area of theology. This variety of approaches reflects the fact that discussion of the practical orientation of theology, no less than any other aspect of theology, cannot be separated from a particular historical and cultural context.

Perhaps the image of a delta, like that of the River Nile as it empties into the Mediterranean, is appropriate to describe the history of the efforts to connect life and theology. Anybody who has viewed a delta from the height of an aircraft will appreciate what this means: there is a swirling assortment of streams that originate from a common source. These tributaries are partially connected, but each is characterized by its own shape and direction, born out of the terrain over which it has flowed. Similarly, the general conviction that theology cannot be separated from practice has been fleshed out in diverse ways, ways that reflect the "terrain" from which the different theologies emerged. Even today, as we shall see, no one articulation of the relationship between faith and life is subscribed to universally.

The diversity of forms that have been used to express the relationship between theology and life demonstrates once again that theology is not something monolithic, that it does not have just one form that must be followed irrespective of the time or the circumstances of its practitioners. Theology is something dynamic, something that has a variety of shapes that cannot be separated from the context out of which they emerge.

This chapter has three aims: to explore some fundamental issues raised by the endeavor to give theology a practical orientation; to illustrate the variety of ways in which this orientation has been articulated throughout the history of theology; and to demonstrate, via the example of the treatment of refugees introduced above, one contemporary application of the practical orientation of theology.

Shaping Theology in Practice: Some Challenges

One of the first issues confronting anyone who investigates the practical orientation of theology is whether this orientation is better regarded as a separate branch of theology, like the theology of the sacraments, or whether it is better regarded as an approach that should characterize theology as a whole. Those who hold the latter view argue that all branches of theology must relate to human experience, must integrate theory and practice, and so be practical. The former point of view claims that the practical dimension of theology, because it has a distinct focus and methodology, is a legitimate and specialized discipline in its own right. Arguments could be advanced to support either side of this argument, but the main point to realize is that both approaches affirm the link between theology and practice.

Just as there has been a debate on how to categorize the emphasis on theology as practical, so too there has been a variety of opinions about how to name this emphasis. The term *practical theology,* which is most commonly used today, is not the only name applied to this kind of theology. *Pastoral theology*—a term derived from the biblical image of a shepherd/pastor—has also been often used to identify this discipline, especially in its relationship to the work of the church's ministers. In addition, we hear increasingly about *theological reflection.* Although this term lacks a precise meaning, it tends to refer to any kind of theological thinking about current experiences, an activity that can and should be done by all members of the church, not just professional theologians. *Ministerial theology* is yet another term used today to refer to the theological reflection that is part of the training of women and men for ministry and is usually done within the setting of supervised "hands-on" or field education.

To overcome any possible confusion that might arise from this plethora of terms, in this chapter we will refer to *practical theology* as that specialized discipline of theology that deals with Christian reflec-tion in the service of the church and society. It is the discipline that links theory and practice. The concerns of practical theology are not confined to the church, much less to the activity of the ordained minis-ters of the church, but they relate also to Christianity's contribution to the wider world. Practical theology, therefore, is concerned with what it means to believe and act as Christians within the world of our experi-ence: "Practical theology raises the question of the presence of the Kingdom of God in our history."[1] Practical theology, therefore, is insep-arable from any endeavor to do theology.

Within practical theology, the relationship between the Christian tradition (especially the Bible and the church's teaching) and the insights gained from one's experiences of life and forms of secular knowledge such as biology, anthropology, psychology, sociology, and political science is a matter of some tension. This tension can be illus-trated by a number of key questions: Should either Christian tradition or the human sciences take precedence for the Christian in decision making? How do the insights from each influence the other? We can demonstrate the force of such questions by examining how they might apply in the context of divorce: How do the biblical texts dealing with divorce relate to our modern-day experience and understanding of human relationships and the changing social conditions of marriage itself? How does a particular couple come to a decision on separation and remarriage in light of their own particular story, circumstances, and faith commitments? What options ought be open to them after the breakdown of their marriage? Questions like these are of vital interest to practical theology.

The focus of practical theology is another contentious point: Should it be exclusively about church-related matters, or should it also be con-cerned with the broader issues that face our society? Similarly, there is the question of whether practical theology ought to be focused on matters that pertain to the experiences of specific individuals or whether it ought to deal with more global issues such as world hunger, global-warming, and the preservation of our forests. Once again, different approaches to practi-cal theology will resolve these issues in different ways.

The fact that there are various responses to the issues raised above, as well as the fact that practical theology is not the exclusive preserve of people of any one gender or cultural background (the different "terrains" referred to above) means that it is increasingly appropriate to talk of practical theologies, rather than simply practical theology. One result of this diversity is that theology now has a more local than global focus. Such local theologies give priority to criteria drawn from the cultural or political experience of particular groups, rather than to the more traditional academic and, usually, male-dominated categories that presented themselves as timeless and independent of any one culture.[2] This development means that the theologies, the prayers, and the liturgies produced by, for example, groups of women or indigenous people who have been marginalized in their own country will clearly be different from those shaped primarily by male academics.

The development of local theologies is an expression of the pluralism in contemporary theology discussed in chapter 1. The fact that, in its practical orientation as much as anywhere else, contemporary theology is irreducibly pluralist can be a source of anxiety for people who fear that it will splinter Christianity. Although it is important that such a danger not be ignored, it would also be wrong not to affirm the value of pluralism, not to affirm that it reflects the desire of people from a variety of backgrounds to engage in theology. Pluralism, in theory and practice, does raise the issue of how the Christian community preserves its unity in faith; but pluralism also demonstrates that God's revelation is for all people and therefore can be appropriated in a variety of ways.

In order to appreciate how this pluralism in practical theology has come about, we need to survey the history of the various ways in which Christians have sought to unite faith and practice.

Practical Theology: Historical Foundations

In this section we will consider some aspects of the history of what we would now term practical theology. The focus will be on the evolution of practical theology from the beginnings of Christianity until the end of the Second Vatican Council.

From Early Christianity to the Reformation

Although the term *theology* was not commonly used in early Christianity, theology as a reflection upon God and the life of faith was, as we have seen in various places throughout this book, a common practice within the first Christian communities. The theology produced in the centuries that followed the formation of the New Testament, theology produced by people like Justin, Athanasius, and John Chrysostom, who are included in the group known as the Fathers of the Church, was designed to meet immediate pastoral needs. Accordingly, this theology took the form of homilies, arguments against the critics of Christian belief, liturgies, instruction of candidates for baptism, responses to those who had abandoned their faith, commentaries on the Bible, instruction on the sacraments, guidance in asceticism for monks, and even reactions to barbarian invaders who overthrew Christian institutions.

The purpose of this theology was to develop faith through ordered knowledge and a proper emotional disposition toward God, others, and creation; it aimed to develop a habit or disposition within the human soul of the believer. Even the most speculative reflections were directed toward the practical end of nurturing and defending the faith. As such, all theology at this time could be considered practical theology. Because the truth of the revealed texts of the Bible was assumed, the task of Christian thought was to discern and properly formulate its meaning for the life of the church.[3] Theology in these early centuries of the Christian church was not considered to be abstract or impersonal; it was a knowledge of God for the purpose of gaining salvation.

As monasticism developed in Europe from the sixth century on, the monasteries became the home of theology with the result that theology and spirituality were closely linked. But by the latter part of the twelfth century, theology had moved to the emerging cosmopolitan universities in the great urban centers of medieval Europe, places like Paris, Bologna, Oxford, and Salamanca. In the universities, theology came to be understood and practiced along the lines of an Aristotelian model, a theoretical science alongside other disciplines such as law, medicine, and the liberal arts. As the tradition of the universities developed, theology not only evolved into an academic discipline studied for its own sake, but it also became more speculative.

In this environment, the practical orientation of theology was no longer understood as applying to the whole of theology, but was understood as simply one aspect of the broader theological enterprise that became known as *Scholasticism* and was derived largely from the theology of Thomas Aquinas. Theology as a rigorous and well-ordered science now belonged to the universities. Theology as a practical discipline did not disappear, but was marginalized, emerging principally as devotional or spiritual theology linked with monastic life. Theology's practical concern was therefore largely apart from the world. Consequently, doctrinal analysis and reflection on Christian living became further and further separated.

Martin Luther and the Protestant Reformers reacted against these developments. For Luther, theology was practical; it was intimately bound up with the fostering of faith aimed at a total and trustful commitment of the self to God. John Calvin systematized Protestant beliefs into a scholarly treatise known as the *Institutes,* in which he was at pains to demonstrate theology's practical application to matters pertaining to salvation. As in Catholicism, Protestant theology eventually became increasingly split into two camps: a highly speculative theology associated with the university, and a more practical, spiritual theology linked with evangelical pietism. In both Catholicism and Protestantism, therefore, practical theology became the devotional or spiritual genre of theological activity.

Practical Theology as Moral Theology

A further development of theology as a practical discipline within Catholic circles came as a result of its association with the sacrament of penance and the role of the confessor in that sacrament. The way for this development had been prepared by the Fourth Lateran Council in 1215, which made mandatory the once-a-year reception of the Eucharist, together with an annual confession of sins to an approved priest as a preparation for the Eucharist. It was after the Council of Trent that the role of the confessor took on greater importance. Trent directed that the diocesan clergy, in order to enable them to fulfill their duty as confessors, were to be better educated. In his role as confessor, the priest was to instruct the penitent about how to be virtuous and to offer some form of spiritual direction, however minimal. The confessor's predominant role, however, was to be that of a judge: he was to assess the sinfulness of the matters confessed by the penitent. From this requirement arose the need to find practical solutions to difficult problems of conscience, to establish if and to what degree a person had sinned. This pastoral need gave rise to moral texts for clergy and to the theological activity known as "moral theology," an activity that relied substantially on canon law.

Practical Theology as Pastoral Theology

Just as moral theology was the product of a particular need of the church's ordained ministry, so "pastoral theology" considered theology in practice as primarily the study associated with the work of assisting people to acquire the skills and personal qualities needed for pastoral care ministry within the church. This approach, which arose as an independent subject in German-speaking Catholic theological schools in the late eighteenth century, was for the training of priests, who were regarded as the sole agents of the church's pastoral ministry.[4] The Second Vatican Council's Decree on the Training of Priests, *Optatam Totius,* understood pastoral theology in this way when it stated,

> *That pastoral concern which should characterize the whole formation program also requires that students be especially trained in what is relevant to the sacred ministry, that is, in catechesis and preaching, liturgy and administration of the sacraments, works of charity, meeting the needs of those in error and of unbelievers, and in all other pastoral duties. Let them be carefully trained in the art of directing souls. (OT 19)*

Such a pastoral theology arose from a clerical paradigm that is concerned with the skills needed for nurturing the inner life of the church. In terms of the education of candidates for the ordained ministry, this approach focused on the specific tasks involved in learning the skills required for teaching, preaching, administration, pastoral care, and so on. It was the practical application of the different branches of theology: moral theology, canon law, biblical studies, and sacramental theology.

Vatican II appears to reflect this understanding of practical theology as a theology of application confined to church ministry:

> *Theological subjects should be taught in the light of faith under the guidance of the Church's magisterium so that students will accurately draw Catholic teaching from divine revelation, enter deeply into its meaning, use it to nourish their spiritual lives and be able to proclaim, explain and defend it in their priestly ministry....Let*

them also learn to use the light of divine revelation in seeking the
solution to human problems, to apply its eternal truths to the
changing condition of human life, and to communicate these truths
in a way the modern world can understand. (OT 16)

The passage quoted understands theology in practice—pastoral
theology—as a discipline designed to equip those engaged in church
ministry with the competence, skills, and spiritual qualities and dispo-
sitions needed to carry out their task.

Practical Theology Since Vatican II

Ecclesial Theology

Innovation in the understanding of practical theology after Vatican II, as in so many other areas in the life of the church, was largely
the result of the impetus provided by Karl Rahner, who was instrumental in the development of a new style of pastoral theology that was more
than spiritual theology, moral theology, or the application of ministerial
skills. For Rahner, practical theology was especially concerned both
with the structures of the church, rather than the study of the activities
of the individual minister, and with the church's response to the contemporary needs of our world. Rahner emphasized that the church must
ever be alert to the present moment: practical theology is the theological perception of the present moment in relation to the church carrying
out its mission.

In its ecclesial form, practical theology would seek to understand,
for example, the religious indifference of people in Western societies
and the impact it has on the church. It would make use of psychological
and social analysis in its efforts to answer questions like, Why have so
many people apparently abandoned Christianity in search of new
meanings? The implications could then be drawn as to how the church
at different levels—the parish, the diocese, a nation—could effectively
restructure institutions and forms of ministry to meet this present
moment of the world's history. Similarly, the current theological debate
concerning the ministry of women can take the form of a practical theology that considers the Bible and the church's tradition, but tests them
against the changing social role of women in modern society, the new
self-understanding of women generated by feminism, and the current

needs within the community to which a ministry of women might respond. Practical theology in its ecclesial form attempts

> *to be of service in continually overcoming the Church's given defi-*
> *cient self-realization and transcending it in the next new form to*
> *which the Church is being called.*[5]

This understanding of practical theology was extensively developed in *Handbuch der Pastoraltheologie,* a five-volume work coedited by Rahner, which appeared in the 1960s and included the work of educationalists, psychologists, and sociologists.[6] The authors stressed that the findings of the secular sciences and our knowledge of history and culture must be examined from the perspective of theology. The aim was to provide a concrete, practical theology of the church.

This understanding of practical theology within the Catholic tradition is also illustrated by thinkers like the French theologian Yves Congar, whose pioneering work helped to pave the way for the reforms of Vatican II. Congar affirmed the secularity of the lay person as being a positive and necessary contribution to the life and mission of the church. The particular responsibility of lay people is to keep the secular world oriented toward the kingdom of God.[7]

In this historical survey, we must not overlook a movement that altered the shape of the church in the middle years of the twentieth century: *Catholic Action.* Unlike Congar's understanding of the lay person's vocation as a vocation in its own right arising from baptism, the practical theology behind Catholic Action regarded the lay apostolate as inspired, defined, and controlled by the bishops, the church's hierarchy. Yet, despite this limited perspective, it was a force for the church's renewal. Catholic Action had two goals: first, the spiritual, moral, and theological formation of its members; and second, the spread of Christ's kingdom in the world. It encouraged people to carry the gospel into the workplace, and in some countries it took on a political form as it encouraged Catholics to organize themselves to counter the influence of Communism in the trade unions. It was the sort of theology that inspired Cardinal Suhard's writings and pastoral initiatives as Archbishop of Paris in the 1940s as he came to the realization that this immense, urban diocese had ceased to be truly Christian. Similarly, the Young Christian Workers (YCW), founded by Cardinal Cardijn in Belgium, was a result of the practical theology behind Catholic Action based on three principles: *See, Judge, and Act.*

After Catholic Action and the Young Christian Workers, the most significant boost to a rethinking of the ecclesial dimension of practical theology came, not surprisingly, from the Second Vatican Council. In *Lumen Gentium,* the Dogmatic Constitution on the Church, the initial image of the church presented is that of the whole people of God, a community out of which flows the hierarchy and offices in the church. In addition, the council, by its endorsement of coresponsibility, new ministries, collaboration, and creative methods of evangelization, erected the theological framework for the way the Catholic Church saw itself and its mission in the years that followed.

The revised Rite of Christian Initiation of Adults (RCIA)—the liturgical, catechetical, and pastoral program for receiving new members into the church—which was published in 1972, came to be seen as a model for all pastoral care and catechesis. Its theological foundations emphasize conversion, the reading of the scriptures, liturgy, the listening to and telling of life stories, and a sharing of ministries that embrace the entire Christian community. It has arisen out of a practical theology of evangelization and sacraments that has given new shape and vitality to the contemporary church.

To sum up, from the ecclesial perspective, practical theology aims to assist the church in reflecting upon its never-ending need to be reborn in new cultural and historical circumstances. It goes beyond a clerical or education-for-ministry model to a far broader vision of the church's structures and mission.

Theology of Pastoral Counseling

Pastoral counseling, which draws on the psychological theories of human personality and communication skills and which emerged principally from mainstream North American Protestantism, has had a profound influence on Catholic practical theology in the last three decades. The origins of this approach are to be found in the work of Anton Boisen and the Clinical Pastoral Education movement (CPE). As chaplain at the Worcester State Hospital in Massachusetts, Boisen conducted the first program of CPE in the summer of 1925. Student chaplains in this psychiatric hospital kept detailed written records of their observations, conversations, and subsequent reflections upon patients. These were then analyzed in a small group that sought to bring together the disciplines of religion, theology, psychology, medicine, and social work for the purpose of the improved pastoral care of patients. The empirical study of the patient's needs and the reactions of the chaplain provided the material to theologize upon and evaluate ministry—the clinical approach to pastoral care. This method gave rise to a practical theology based on what came to be called "the living document," namely, the person who is the patient.

Although the medical setting with its wide range of patients who could be visited easily continued as a locus for CPE, the program found that its methods could be adapted to other pastoral settings, including prisons, parishes, and schools. The ability to think theologically about concrete ministry and the intrapersonal and interpersonal skills acquired were seen to be readily transferable to other areas of ministry.

In the early history of the pastoral counseling approach to practical theology, psychology was the dominant partner. The Bible and the Christian tradition provided little more than religious sanction and blessing to the secular sciences. More recently, however, a shift has occurred to give greater emphasis to the resources from the wisdom of the Christian tradition. As a result, this approach to theology and ministry has become more theological, and counseling is not seen as the only model of pastoral care. There is also a shift beyond an exclusive focus on crisis ministry; in its place, there is the desire to foster growth within Christian living. Spirituality and ethics are seen as critical factors in pastoral care and reflection. There is an attempt to demonstrate how the common concerns and problems of people can be placed within the context of spiritual themes like the need for faith, repentance, vocation, and the desire for communion. Theological issues are seen to be at the heart of pastoral care, even when it is expressed in secular language. Thus, the experiences of ministry give rise to the possibility of a rich and enabling practical theology, aided by the insights of the psychological sciences.

Liberation Theology

The liberation approach to theology in practice originated amid the misery and oppression found among the poor in much of Latin America and quickly spread to other countries in similar circumstances, like the

Philippines. Liberation theology stresses the importance of bringing human experience into real dialogue with the Christian tradition. It enables us to understand the meaning of faith in new and previously unrecognized ways. The starting point of any theology must always be the lives of individuals and communities, especially their oppression in its many forms. Liberation theology, as a form of practical theology, is about changing society. It is social rather than individualistic in its orientation. It has recovered the social dimension of sin, conversion, and grace; and it reads the scriptures from the perspective of society's victims. Liberation from all forms of bondage is salvation; hence, the transformation of society from social structures of sin to a state of justice as willed in God's kingdom is more than a secular process. It is nothing less than God's redemptive presence at work in the world.

What are the features of liberation theology? There is a "deprivatization" of the gospel: its message is not merely personal but social. This theology is not concerned with a rational interpretation of the world, but with a desire to change it. Truth statements can only be judged in their relationship to liberating praxis, which is action informed by reflection. There is a "preferential option" for the poor and oppressed groups within society. Theology has the task of uncovering the ideologies present in religion and the social order. Theology itself, then, is a political act. Finally, although assisted by academic theologians, liberation theology emerges from, and belongs to, the oppressed themselves. This is the reason for the importance given to basic ecclesial communities as the place where pastoral care and the continuing cycle of Christian reflection upon action occurs. It is a practical theology in which all can participate.

The critics of liberation theology allege that it relies too heavily on a Marxist interpretation of reality. In response to this critique, the Brazilian theologian Leonardo Boff acknowledges that liberation theology runs the risk of ignoring the need for personal conversion and of allowing politics and economic theory to dim the horizon of faith, but he also emphasizes that "thanks to this theology, interest in theological reflection has reached the streets. It is a theology that is powerfully prophetic and missionary."[8]

As we have mentioned, liberation theology has been taken up by other oppressed groups as a method of doing theology with the purpose of changing social attitudes and practice. These groups include black people, women, the aged, the handicapped, gays and lesbians, and environmentalists.

A variant of the liberation approach to practical theology is "contextual theology," which stresses how theology will look different according to the culture in which it takes place.[9] This approach allows not only the asking of new questions, but also asking questions that past frameworks of theology are unable to answer. Context shapes reflection. For example, the experience of being a Christian in a predominantly Buddhist culture such as Thailand will give rise to new questions and theological responses to religious pluralism: can Christianity continue to think of itself in exactly the same way when it comes to such matters as salvation or ways to holiness? Of course, this is not new. The Christian religion demonstrated itself to be remarkably adaptive when it moved beyond the confines of Judaism to the Graeco-Roman world. It completely transformed its understandings of the person of Jesus in light of the new context of Greek philosophical thought in which it found itself. Today churches in the Third World are no longer content to repeat a merely European/North American experience and understanding of the gospel.

Practical theology of the liberation variety always begins with human experience within the context of social injustice. It takes seriously the values of contemporary society and secular knowledge. It is about social change. The timeless words of the Bible are living, continuously contextualized into the current situation, and read in new ways. It is a democratic kind of theology, for all are invited to engage in it, to learn from each other. It is not just for the specialists. It is a theology of action, which is meant to disturb and transform institutionalized injustice.

In our survey of the history of approaches to practical theology, we have concentrated not just on the differences between the various models, but on the reasons for those differences. We have seen that the differences reflect the context—the situation of the church, the principal cultural influences, the particular view of the relationship between God's action in the world and the human response—out of which a theology emerges. We have also seen that the different theologies are, not surprisingly, dissimilar in their response to the issues we identified early on as the main challenges to practical theology, such as the relationship between theology and the human sciences and whether practical theology should focus only on church-related issues or should have a broader agenda. Diversity in practical theologies is thus a reflection of the diversity in background of those who do practical theology. The diverse theologies, however, do share a commitment to action.

A Method of Practical Theology

The final task of this chapter is to explore one method that can guide our efforts to put theology into practice: "critical correlation." Its foundations have been expressed best by the contemporary American theologian David Tracy. Tracy emphasizes that theology finds its two principal sources in the Christian tradition and in common human experience and language. It is these sources that are to be brought into a mutual critical correlation. Theology can begin from either direction: from experience or from Christian tradition. Experience, argues Tracy, is human experience only to the extent that it is interpreted. Likewise the Christian tradition, which is radically ambiguous, is never exempt from the need for interpretation. A hermeneutics of the tradition must not only involve retrieval, but also critique; it must utilize a "hermeneutics of suspicion." In its application to the Christian tradition, this method would look for the distortions that have resulted from such things as racism, sexism, elitism, individualism, and anti-Semitism.

Tracy stresses that while practical theology is influenced and guided by other branches of theology, it can also guide and influence them. Practical theology, he argues, must be geared to a changing society.[10] In its commitment to change in society and to a self-critical attitude within the church, the critical correlation method reflects many of the concerns raised by Rahner in the decade after Vatican II. It also expresses the priorities of liberationist and feminist theologians.

What does the methodology of critical correlation look like? Such a practical theology follows what has become known as the "pastoral cycle." Although a number of distinct models of the pastoral cycle have emerged in the practical theology books, with minor variations in emphases they generally follow five broad steps: (1) beginning with a description of a concrete *life experience* and the feelings this evokes within us; (2) examining what our *culture* can teach us about the issue under discussion—society's values and practices, social sciences, other sources of knowledge, media presentation, and so on; (3) discovering what the *Christian tradition* can offer us about this experience—for example, the Bible, the church's teachings, theology, liturgy, spirituality, ethics, and the church's practice; (4) analyzing how these three poles of knowledge can influence each other in order to produce new insights into the issue under examination—*exploration* (this involves not only the interpretation and uncovering of social, religious, and historical bias, but also social analysis of the causes and consequences of beliefs and actions; this step helps to make sense of experiences, sources of cultural knowledge, and religious beliefs by putting a pluralism of ideas into a broader picture and making connections; it is the process of pastoral theologizing); (5) making decisions as a result of this theological process—*action.* Other possible responses can be suggested, for there is not always a clear solution and course of action.

The pastoral cycle is really a spiral as it continues through further reflection, so that a final point is not reached, but decisions remain open to further investigation. The pastoral cycle also presumes that our understandings are contextualized and ever open to new understandings and interpretations.

We will now illustrate what this method of critical correlation looks like in practice. Imagine again that you are part of an ecumenical group from a neighborhood cluster of churches who have come together to make a contribution to the debate about the treatment of refugees. This group will make use of the five-step process of the pastoral cycle described above. (It is worth noting that this method could equally be used by an individual Christian, a professional practical theologian, a small group, or a broad community consultation; practical theology, in other words, can be done at different levels and in a variety of settings.)

The first step, the description of *life experience,* might begin by reflecting on our personal experience of refugees in the community, the thoughts and feelings their presence evokes within us at a community level: What is happening among refugees in our community? Is there discrimination? Do we know what is being done for their welfare? How are people responding to their presence? Answers to these questions that arise from the community's experience need to be thought about, discussed, and summarized. A number of refugees, of different ages and backgrounds, might provide information by making known their experiences and needs within this local community. Representatives from the community's service organizations might also report on their dealings with refugee issues.

The second step in the process of theological reflection is to concern ourselves with *cultural* knowledge. Questions that we can ask include: Why are people displaced? What international and national efforts are being made to assist these displaced persons? What are the current laws and practices in our country concerning refugees? How is the media portraying this matter? Does the United Nations have a set of principles concerning refugees and their care? Has there been a change in social attitudes toward refugees in our community? Can we learn anything from social theory about the plight of displaced people?

The third step in practical theology is to examine our *Christian tradition:* What biblical material can we draw upon concerning refugees and society's response? Have there been any statements from the leadership of the churches on this matter? What are our understandings of Christian social justice principles? What is meant by the church's teaching of "a preferential option for the poor"? How have Christians in the past responded to displaced persons?

The fourth step in the process is that of *exploration* and analysis: How do these three sources of knowledge above interact with one another? Does our Christian tradition challenge current social attitudes or government policies? Is the church at the national and local level sufficiently involved? Are attitudes or teachings in our church community in need of change in the light of what has been learned from our cultural analysis?

Finally, there is *action.* Reflection must precede and guide action: what can we do as a local community? A practical theology leads to practical action. Possible actions are identified and evaluated. For example, the group might ask whether it is possible to initiate an education program to inform and change attitudes, to lobby at the political level for greater access within this community to certain social services, or to provide some kind of practical help in housing and language assistance in the local community.

The action that takes place will, inevitably, give rise to new experiences and new questions, which become the raw material for further reflection and further dialogue with the tradition. Thus, action should be understood not simply as the end of the cycle, but as the catalyst that begins a new cycle, a new cycle that will produce new action. The link between action and further reflection illustrates why the pastoral cycle can be understood as a spiral: the process continues but always from a new starting point, a starting point produced by the action that resulted from the previous cycle.

Conclusion

It is heartening to know that in recent years many people in positions of leadership in the church have taken to doing practical theology in this way when engaging in a public teaching role. In countries like the United States, Canada, Great Britain, Australia, and New Zealand, conferences of bishops and national church councils have issued detailed pastoral statements on subjects as diverse as the economy, peace and war, marriage and the family, the role of women, sexuality, and the environment. In the preparation of these documents, a serious dialogue has taken place: the experience of people has been listened to; efforts have been made to understand the subject under discussion from a variety of viewpoints by inviting contributions to the discussion from people with different kinds of expertise and experience within and beyond the church; scriptural themes and Christian theological thinking have been explored and brought into interaction with ideas gained from elsewhere. The process adopted has been public and participatory. The documents that have resulted from such processes are designed to seek transformation within the church and the wider society. In addition, the plurality of opinions has been respected and the decisions and recommended courses of action are sometimes recognized as tentative and not the last word.

Practical theology is now a specialized and professional discipline. Increasingly, it is gaining respectability as a field of study in its own right within academic institutions. Alongside the biblical scholar, the ethicist, and the systematic theologian, there is now the practical theologian. As an all-embracing term for describing theology in practice, "practical theology" has replaced "pastoral theology" as the preferred terminology, for in its study, it reaches beyond the confines of the church to include engagement with the wider world, which is the venue for the kingdom of God.

Yet practical theology can never be the exclusive possession of the professional. Practical theology is also the work of the whole Christian community as it engages in theological reflection. Liberation theology, as we have seen, has demonstrated that theology belongs to all the people of God, since its starting point is the experience of women, men, and children within the context of their own lives. The scholar needs the people and the people need the scholar. Practical theology, therefore, can be an activity carried out at different levels—by individuals, groups, and communities. It is, above all, participatory theology. It is a theology that starts with the concrete reality of where people are. It is a theology that begins with praxis and ends in praxis. It is a theology of dialogue. It does not presume that any one group has all the answers. It does not follow the "teacher and taught" method. Individuals, the church, and society learn from each other. Each challenges the biases and limitations of the other in order to reach renewed understandings and behaviors that will contribute to a better quality of life for all people, so that all might live in hope.

QUESTIONS FOR REFLECTION

1. What are the strengths and weaknesses of each of the approaches to practical theology described in this chapter?

2. What makes practical theology different from systematic theology or ethics?

3. What are some of the different settings in which practical theology might be done? How would they differ in their approach?

4. Having chosen something from your own life experience, how would you engage in a process of theological reflection on it using the "critical correlation" approach?

SUGGESTIONS FOR FURTHER READING

- Ballard, Paul and John Pritchard. *Practical Theology in Action: Christian Thinking in the Service of Church and Society.* London: SPCK, 1996.

- O'Connell, Patricia Killen and John de Beer. *The Art of Theological Reflection.* New York: Crossroad, 1995.

- Patton, John. *From Ministry to Theology: Pastoral Action and Reflection.* Nashville, Tenn.: Abingdon, 1990.

- Whitehead, James and Evelyn Whitehead. *Method in Ministry.* New York: Seabury, 1981.

NOTES

[1]Paul Ballard and John Pritchard, *Practical Theology in Action* (London: SPCK, 1996), 16.

[2]James M. Byrne, "Theology and Christian Faith," in *Why Theology?* ed. Claude Geffré and Werner Jeanrond, *Concilium* (1994): 6.

[3]Edward Farley, *Theologia: The Fragmentation and Unity of Theological Education* (Philadelphia: Fortress Press, 1983), 34.

[4]Heinz Schuster, "Pastoral Theology: Nature and Function," *Concilium* 3 (1965): 4–9; Heinz Schuster, in *Sacramentum Mundi* s.v. "Pastoral Theology" (New York: Herder & Herder, 1969), 4:365–68.

[5]Karl Rahner, "Practical Theology Within the Totality of Theological Disciplines," in Karl Rahner, *Theological Investigations*, tr. Graham Harrison (London: Darton, Longman & Todd, 1972), 9:104.

[6]F. X. Arnold, F. Klostermann, K. Rahner, V. Schurr and L. Webber, eds., *Handbuch der Pastoraltheologie,* 5 vols. (Freiburg: Herder, 1963–69).

[7]See, for example, Yves Congar, *Lay People in the Church* (London: Bloomsbury, 1957).

[8]Leonardo Boff, *Church, Charism, and Power*, tr. J. W. Diereksmeier (London: SCM, 1985; New York: Crossroad, 1986), 20.

[9]S. B. Bevans, *Models of Contextual Theology* (Maryknoll, N.Y.: Orbis, 1992).

[10]David Tracy, "The Foundations of Practical Theology," in *Practical Theology: The Emerging Field in Theology, Church, and World,* ed. Don S. Browning (San Francisco: Harper & Row, 1983).

EPILOGUE

In the present era of cyber-technology, interactivity is a prized quality. People today do not merely watch passively as they did when television was the most advanced medium, but they seek to influence and shape the "world" on the screen. The discussion in this book has stressed that theology has always been—and remains—interactive. Moreover, theology invites interaction not with holograms, but with the world of flesh-and-blood reality, the world that is the venue for our relationship with God.

In introducing the themes that shape Catholic theology's interaction with the world, we have also highlighted for the reader the fact that theology has a history. This history is important because it clearly shows us the dynamism of theology, a dynamism that has been produced by the meeting of God's self-revelation and the human desire to respond to God. We have seen that the expression of that desire is shaped by the context of those doing theology. Thus, different understandings of, for example, the human person, the structure of society, and even language, have affected the type of theology that is done. We have also acknowledged that the history of theology has been influenced profoundly by the genius of people like Augustine, Thomas Aquinas, and Karl Rahner, who saw themselves not simply as individuals trying to make sense of their individual lives, but as members of the church anxious to help others in their wrestling with the mystery of God.

People of genius have been important in the history of theology, but we have stressed that theology is not elitist. Theology can be done by all people who, on the basis of the questions raised by, and the insights gained from, their own lives, reflect on their faith and seek to know how best to respond to God and their neighbors. This emphasis on experience moves us beyond theory to questions of practice. Thus, we have illustrated how liberation theology, grounded in the experience of poverty and oppression, has been a catalyst for the movement of theology away from the specifically academic world and has grounded theology in the lived experience of people of faith. In addition, we have pointed to the recent emergence of an emphasis on women's experience as the foundation for theology. It is this latter emphasis, perhaps more than any other in modern history, which guarantees that the shape of Catholic theology will continue to change.

The emergence of new platforms from which to do theology is always a test of the capacity of the Christian tradition to grow. This book has depicted that tradition as something alive, as the movement of the Spirit within the church, and therefore as limitless in its capacity for development. In studying theology, we are not simply learning about God and the world, but we are interacting with the God whose Spirit is at the heart of our tradition, and we are being invited to reveal that God to the world. Accepting that invitation is a sign of our hope.

INDEX